THE
POLITICS
OF
CONSCIENCE

THE
POLITICS
OF
CONSCIENCE

**The Historic Peace Churches
and America at War, 1917-1955**

A Christian Peace Shelf Selection

ALBERT N. KEIM and
GRANT M. STOLTZFUS
Foreword by Dean M. Kelley

WIPF & STOCK · Eugene, Oregon

Wipf and Stock Publishers
199 W 8th Ave, Suite 3
Eugene, OR 97401

The Politics of Conscience
The Historic Peace Churches and America at War, 1917-1955
By Keim, Albert N. and Stoltzfus, Grant M.
Copyright© Herald Press
ISBN 13: 9781532666551
Publication date 6/15/2000
Previously published by Herald Press, 1988

*To
the late
Grant M. Stoltzfus,
teacher of history,
lover of peace.*

Contents

Foreword

Those who value freedom of conscience owe a great debt to the historic peace churches. They have led a valiant and effective defense of the right of conscientious objectors not to be compelled to render military service and not to be legally penalized for following the leading of conscience.

Grouped in three venerable families—the Mennonites, the Friends (Quakers), and the Brethren—these pacifist (or nonresistant) Christians have lived out a remarkably faithful witness to their understanding of the Lord's command in the Sermon on the Mount, "Do not resist one who is evil. But if any one strikes you on the right cheek, turn to him the other also" (Matt. 5:38, RSV).

Tribute to this witness was expressed by Justice Oliver Wendell Holmes when he dissented from a decision of the Supreme Court barring naturalization of an alien who refused to promise to bear arms in defense of the nation. He said, "I would suggest that the Quakers have done their share to make the country what it is ... and I had not supposed hitherto that we regretted our inability to expel them because they believe more than some of us do in the teachings of the Sermon on the Mount" (*U.S. v. Schwimmer*, 1929).

Numbering less than half a million adherents, the historic peace churches have kept before the other 240 million of us the vision of a world without war. They have kept the vision of a nation in which those who refuse to take up arms would be respected for their sincere convictions and would be allowed to contribute to the common good without violating those convictions. That interim vision of respect for dissenting conscience is even now (as always) difficult to attain, elusive to share, and precarious to defend.

There are always those who want to sacrifice it for some supposed greater good or more urgent need, such as the representative from Michigan, Paul Shafer, who uttered in 1951 the line for which (alone) he will be remembered, "Might it not be in everyone's best interest to simply put all conscientious objectors in jail?" Too often that has been the course followed by nations which make no pretense of respect for conscience or esteem for religious liberty. Some of these nations we have called "enemies" while emulating their least desirable traits. It has been the not-always-adequately-appreciated gift of the peace churches to keep before us this vision that might lead us beyond the self-defeating toils of enmity to a better way.

It is ironic that within the fragile alliance of the peace churches there arose a tension between those who sought simple deferment and those who wanted to oppose the entire military machinery. This tension intensified in the period of the Vietnam conflict, when conscientious objection was utilized by growing numbers of young men as a way of demonstrating their opposition to national policy in carrying on that war. The tension became even more prominent when the Supreme Court expanded the definition of "religious training and belief" to include nontheistic (*U.S. v. Seeger*, 1965) and then virtually nonreligious (*Welsh v. U.S.* 1970) objectors, but inexplicably refused to exempt clearly religious "just-war" objectors to a particular war (*Negre v. Larsen*, 1971). But that is beyond the time-frame of this book.

This volume describes the basic struggle to obtain a decent accommodation in national policy for the historic peace church conscientious objector who was clearly religious. This type of person objected to participation in any and all wars and did not wish to be part of the military effort in any way, but was willing and ready to render civilian service in "the national health, safety, and interest."

That struggle extended from 1917 to 1955, the period covered by this book. Stoltzfus and Keim have traced the steps of that struggle as the peace churches, seemingly powerless and fragmented novices, learned "from scratch" by trial and error the ways of influencing public policy. With the gifts and perseverance of a number of able and dedicated leaders, they were able to make a vital contribution out of all proportion to their numbers. As the authors rightly observe in conclusion:

> The drive for alternate service for conscientious objectors was a remarkably sustained and focused effort. The historic peace churches had no political leverage. Their constituencies were among the most single-mindedly nonpolitical, nonparticipatory groups in American society. They had few votes. What they did have was a moral and religious conviction embodied in practice.

I had a passing experience with the effectiveness of the peace churches' efforts that I have never forgotten. The ecumenical movement was active in support of conscientious objectors throughout this era, first in the Federal Council of Churches (as the authors indicate) and later in the National Council of Churches, which succeeded it in 1950. We worked closely with the National Service Board for Religious Objectors and even trained draft counselors in the 1960s.

At one point Harold Row of the Church of the Brethren, chairman of the NSBRO, approached me to enlist the support of the National Council of Churches for a further accommodation for conscientious objectors. (I do not now recall what it was.) However, I felt that even with the full support of the main ecumenical body and its 43,000,000 constituents, it would be impossible to budge the hawkish Mendell Rivers, chairman of the House Armed Services Committee. So I told Harold Row I thought it would be a waste of time to try. Nevertheless, he went ahead on this effort and succeeded! Since then I have been careful not to underestimate the power of the historic peace churches when they set about to follow the path of conscience.

So effectively did they follow that path during the years covered by this chronicle that in the I-W program of the early 1950s, they achieved most of what they sought. Moreover, they obtained in the conscription acts of the United States an accepted recognition of conscientious objection to military service that even the "political" use of that provision during the Vietnam conflict did not impugn.

It is for that, as well as for their peace witness as a whole, that all Americans should be grateful to the historic peace churches.

—Dean M. Kelley
National Council of Churches

Author's Preface

This is a history of the efforts of the historic peace churches to create an alternative service for conscientious objectors to war. The forty-year effort began in World War I but it was not until 1955 that the basic elements of a solution were finally completed. The historic peace church conscientious objectors refused all noncombatant service. Their pacifist convictions required freedom from all obligations to serve in any military capacity whatsoever. Hence the search for an alternative service in lieu of military service.

Conscientious objectors are a nuisance to military systems. They "gum up" the system out of all proportion to their numbers. Alternative service offered a means for accommodation between the historic peace churches and the American conscription machinery. But it required many years and vast effort before the accommodation was finally effected.

In American polity conscientious objection is a legislative and political *privilege* rather than a constitutional *right*. Thus the conscientious objector to war is always at risk. He or she can never escape the political exigencies of a particular war or conscription arrangement. The historical context for this situation is more fully developed in chapter one.

This study is narrowly focused on the development of public policy related to alternative service. Thus, at the center of attention are the efforts of the historic peace churches to generate legislative and legal statutes providing for alternative service. Only minimal reference is made to the actual operation of the alternative service programs in operation. Works by Hershberger, Bowman, Gingerich, and others should be consulted for fuller accounts of the Civilian Public Service and I-W programs.

This project was begun more than fifteen years ago by the late Professor Grant Stoltzfus of Eastern Mennonite College. At the time of his untimely death in 1974 he had spent half a decade on research and colleagues of Professor Stoltzfus bequeathed the project to the present writer. My debt to my esteemed former teacher and colleague is only partially satisfied by the joint authorship on the title page. His ideas, research, and inspiration are present throughout the work.

This book, like all such endeavors, is the joint effort of many contributors and institutions. The rich and well-managed archival facilities of the historic peace church community were especially helpful. I must thank the staffs of the American Friends Service Committee Archives in Philadelphia, the Swarthmore College Peace Collection, the Haverford College Library, the Mennonite Historical Library at Goshen College, the Mennonite Archives at Goshen, the Mennonite Library and Archives at Bethel College (Kansas), the Brethren Historical Library and Archives at Elgin (Illinois), and the Menno Simons Historical Library and Archives at Eastern Mennonite College. The

National Archives, the Selective Service Archives, and the National War College Archives at Carlisle, Pennsylvania, were all very helpful at various stages of the work.

I owe particular gratitude to several individuals. Among them Mrs. Ruth Stoltzfus who patiently waited and encouraged me in the slow progress of completing what had been a joyous project in the life of her husband. And to the late M. R. Zigler, whose impatience with my slow progress once erupted into an exhortation, "Get on with the book! I don't have much more time, and I don't know what the interlibrary loan arrangements are in heaven!" To my colleagues, Gerald Brunk, John A. Lapp, Richard Detweiler, Myron Augsburger, James O. Lehman, Robert Kreider, and James Juhnke. And to my dean, Dr. Lela Snyder, who despite a tight budget found a sabbatical grant which has provided time for the completion of the work.

As always, my family, Leanna, Melody, and David—who shared all too many research trips thinly disguised as vacations—deserves special thanks.

—*Albert N. Keim*
Harrisonburg, Virginia

CHAPTER 1

Conscientious Objection
and War
in Historical Perspective

*"No person religiously scrupulous of bearing
arms shall be compelled to render military service in person."*

—James Madison, 1789

War and Conscience

Andrew Carnegie created a ten-million dollar trust fund
in 1910 to promote the abolition of war. "When war is
abolished," he told his trustees, they should then "consider
what is the next most degrading evil."

The effort obviously failed, for only four years later the
world was plunged into the most destructive war in human
history. Nation after nation was swept into war. World War
I was total war, fought not only with guns, but with
government bonds, factory lathes, and farmer's plows.
Powerful propaganda aroused enthusiasm for a "war to
end war" and for making the world "safe for democracy."

That there were dissenters whose consciences forbade

joining the war effort came as a surprise to governments and people on all sides of the conflict. Reliance on war as a means to settle differences among nations seemed to most people a necessary and inevitable, if undesirable, course of action. Objection to war to the point of refusal to participate was not only considered unrealistic, but treasonous—a breach of faith with one's nation and people.

Objection to war on grounds of conscience is not a new idea. Its twentieth-century expression has deep roots in the past. Abstention from military service was a hallmark of the early Christians. According to Roland Bainton it was due to a compunction against killing and not to civic irresponsibility. Evidence of this is found in the witness of Tertullian in A.D. 211. When Christians refused to engage in military service, they apparently assumed a role in public service such as transporting mail or taking custody of prisoners.

Fire protection and peacekeeping assignments in Rome were the obligations of the "vigiles." Christians were often found in branches of this form of public service.[1] However, C. J. Cadoux claims that "no Christian ever thought of enlisting in the army after his conversion until the reign of Marcus Aurelius (160 to 180 A.D.)."[2]

As time went on the Christians became Romans and the Romans became Christians. The emergence of the "just war" theory "baptized" warfare. Pax Romana and Pax Christiana began a long, if sometimes uneasy, synthesis. Augustine's tight-knit theory of the just war—based on Hebrew history, classical politics, and Christian apocalypticism—was to become a bulwark for defending a political empire which was assuredly of the City of God.

To be sure the theory was tempered by Christian restraints: no Christian could fight in an unjust war and

there was to be no unnecessary violence, no looting of
temples, no atrocities, and no reprisals. Only those duly authorized were to take life; clergy and monks were forbid-
den to go to war.

This view continued for centuries and is today the
essence of the war ethic of most Christian groups. Im-
plicitly, of course, it contains an alternative to war; if the
war to be waged is an unjust war, the Christian alternative
is not to participate. Unfortunately very few Christians
through the centuries have rejected war on the grounds
that it was unjust. Virtually all wars have been "just" wars.

A further departure from early Christian pacifism was
the crusade or "holy war" of medieval times. This was
epitomized in Pope Urban's famous address in 1095 to the
Franks—a subtle blend of moral advice, atrocity tales, and
appeals to ethnic, cultural, and religious emotions. Though
the crusades against the Muslims were less than successful,
the residue of a militant Christianity remains today.

Mennonite Nonresistance

To trace the history of Christian pacifism into modern
times, a leap of a thousand years must be made from the
early centuries to those precursors of the Reformation who
in renewing a voluntary Christianity began the revival of
nonparticipation in warfare. Rebelling against a church
they considered worldly, they formed new fellowships
which repudiated war. In the case of Peter Waldo—who
was excommunicated—there was also a witness to the
gospel of poverty among his followers. John Wycliffe did
not unreservedly condemn war, but he did reject the
church as a coercive body. His followers helped to shatter

the long-standing ideals of Augustine's City of God.

Only a small minority of the Reformation groups stood for a pacifism based on the spirit of primitive Christianity—the Anabaptists dating from 1525 in Switzerland—the forerunners of the Mennonites. The Mennonites—named after a Dutch priest, Menno Simons, who joined the movement in 1536—survive to the present. During their 450 years of history they suffered frequently for their refusal to participate in warfare. Martyred by Catholic and Protestant states alike, they learned early that toleration for a thoroughgoing pacifism was rare. Their history has been marked by two main streams of migrations in search of religious liberty: from Prussia to Russia and from Russia to the United States, Canada, and South America; and from Switzerland to Germany to colonial America.

The Amish—a well-known American religious sect of Swiss-German stock—are historically a branch of the Mennonites. They arose in Europe in the late 1600s as a protest against the tendency of the Mennonites in Switzerland and Germany to relinquish certain separatistic practices. Since coming to America in the 1700s they have settled in compact and prosperous agricultural communities where they retain Old World folk ways and a thoroughgoing pacifist way of life. In all American wars they have comprised a solid block of pacifist resistance. Their well-known opposition to the compulsory Social Security system is of one piece with their opposition to compulsory military service.

Quaker Pacifism

During the mid-seventeenth century Puritan revolution in England a pacifist-oriented movement led by George

Fox became known as the Society of Friends (Quakers). Emerging in a setting of political and religious intolerance, the Society was a protest against the Protestant majority which Fox believed had compromised on basic Christian principles. One of those principles was peace—the obligation of the Christian to live "in the virtue of that life and power that took away the occasion of all wars."

The Quaker objection to war was based as much on feeling and intuition as it was on rational arguments or scriptural authority. Fox stressed the "Light Within"—something not quite the same as conscience but rather "that which shines into conscience."

Combined with this mystical understanding of the Christian faith was deep reverence for human personality of which the classic formula was Fox's: "There is that of God in every man." This first principle of Quakerism was to become a basic tenet from which flowed many Quaker enterprises in subsequent generations: concern for prisoners and for the humane treatment of the mentally ill, protest of slave traffic, education of freedmen, education for women, and in the twentieth century, systematic relief and reconstruction on an international scale.

The Quaker conviction that human life is sacred and that evil should be challenged and transformed meant that the power of love and goodwill must find a method. Since war epitomizes evil, the Quaker peace testimony has become conspicuous as a derivative of the basic belief in the imminent transcendence of God and the infinite worth of every human being. The forging of alternative service for conscientious objectors to war in the United States and Great Britain in the two world wars owes much to these Quaker tenets.

Quakers have been present on nearly every battlefront since the late 1600s. They were active in relief work in the Irish war of 1690 and cared for sufferers during the siege of Boston in the American Revolution. They aided Greek refugees in the Greco-Turkish war of 1828 and educated the ex-slaves during and after the American Civil War. Many of these activities were spontaneous, not an organized work of the Society.

In the wake of the Franco-German war of 1870-71, however, such activities became an official part of the corporate life of the Society of Friends. By 1914 the Society had come to see itself cast in the role of a healer of the wounds of war. They were standing in the tradition of one of its eminent founders, William Penn, who said, "True godliness does not turn men out of the world, but enables them to live better in it and excite their endeavors to mend it."

Church of the Brethren Pacifism

A third pacifist group to persist into the twentieth century is the Church of the Brethren founded in 1708 in the German village of Schwarzenau. Led by a former pastor in the German Reformed Church, Alexander Mack, the Brethren were also a protesting body seeking to restore primitive Christianity. Claiming no creed but the New Testament, they espoused peace as a fundamental principle. Peace for them was threefold: opposition to war, no coercion in religion, and no litigation in court. The Brethren migrated to the United States in the eighteenth century and are now the most numerous of the three groups.

Though separated in time and origin by centuries (Mennonites in the sixteenth, Quakers in the seventeenth, and Brethren in the eighteenth), diverse in geographical origin, and differing in certain interpretations of the Christian faith, these three groups have developed parallel communities characterized by disciplined group life and corresponding economic behavior. In the seventeenth and eighteenth centuries, Penn's colony on the Delaware became a haven for many oppressed groups. The passenger ship lists of the 1700s are replete with the names of Friends, Brethren, and Mennonites—all of pacifist conviction. Thus colonial Pennsylvania became a seedbed in the New World for the transplantation of Old World pacifism.

Since 1935 the three groups have become known as the "historic peace churches." Interacting in their own ways with the American environment, each group has developed educational and charitable institutions. In both world wars their young men constituted the large majority of conscientious objectors. In World War I the Society of Friends designed and implemented a program of alternative service in foreign relief and construction. At the outset of World War II, the historic peace churches cooperated in an alternative service for conscientious objectors known as Civilian Public Service. With the onset of the Cold War in the late 1940s, a new program of alternative service was begun, building on the experience of the previous decades of interaction and cooperation.

Conscientious Objection and the Constitution

Alternative service for twentieth-century conscientious objectors in England and America was not easily achieved.

Seen in retrospect, the search for an alternative for conscientious objectors to war has been an agonizing ordeal for governments, churches, and all those who cherish and defend civil liberties.

The problem of how to treat the conscientious objector began early in American history. The travail of the twentieth-century conscientious objector is not a product of the all-embracing character of modern warfare. As Paul Russo has cogently pointed out, American constitutional arrangements regarding the bearing of arms by citizens have complicated the matter.[3]

James Madison, member from Virginia to the first session of the First Congress in 1789, brought a number of proposed amendments to the Constitution which became known as the Bill of Rights. Among his proposals was one he felt strongly about.

> The right of the people to keep and bear arms shall not be infringed; a well-armed and well-regulated militia being the best security of a free country; but no person religiously scrupulous of bearing arms shall be compelled to render military service in person.[4]

Madison believed, argues Russo, that conscientious objection should be protected by the Constitution.

But there was vigorous debate, for as Congressman Benson put it, conscientious objection might be a religious conviction, but it could not be construed as a natural right. Hence the argument was made that the matter should be left to the "humanity" of the legislature rather than enshrined as a constitutional right.

Nevertheless, the House of Representatives passed the

amendment by a small majority. The Senate, however, did not approve the action of the House. Thus, the conscientious objector clause of what shortly became the second amendment to the Constitution was lost. According to Russo, the intention of the framers of the second amendment is clear: Congress has control over the conscientious objector to war as one aspect of its general power over military affairs. The legal status of the conscientious objector is derived as a matter of privilege from Congress. In American policy, conscientious objection is a matter of legislative *privilege* rather than Constitutional *right*.

The treatment of the conscientious objector thus becomes a legislative and political matter,. and to the managers of the machinery of war, a time-consuming nuisance. In the course of time an uneasy and tentative resolution of the matter was achieved through provision for alternative service for the conscientious objector. The essential elements of that resolution were only achieved in 1940—a product of compromise and necessity—hammered out legislatively and administratively in the vortex of World War II, but driven by the well-preserved memory of the unsatisfactory treatment of conscientious objectors in previous American wars.

Conscientious Objection in the Civil War

The United States first experienced mass conscription during the Civil War. In March 1863 Congress assumed from the states the entire administration of conscription. The original act provided an exemption for anyone who furnished a satisfactory substitute or provided a $300 commutation fee. But the injustice of the proviso quickly manifested itself. Less than a year later, in February 1864, the Act was amended to recognize only conscientious objectors who were members of religious denominations whose "rules and articles of faith and practise" prohibited them from military service. The secretary of war could assign them to duty in military hospitals, to take care of a freedman, or to pay a fee of $300 for the benefit of sick and wounded soldiers. The payment of the $300 fee was the only provision ever carried out.[5]

In the Confederacy, the draft law of 1862 exempted Quakers, Brethren, Nazarenes, and Mennonites, with the understanding that they would hire a substitute or pay a tax of $500 to the Confederate treasury. The historic peace churches found these conditions severe and often violated. A number of Mennonites and Brethren were imprisoned and a Church of the Brethren leader in the Shenandoah Valley was shot to death by masked men.[6]

The Civil War provisions for conscientious objectors were clearly unsatisfactory. Thus when the crisis of 1914 erupted into war, few precedents existed and the peace churches not only lacked coordinated organizations, they had not given much thought to the problem of the conscientious objector in wartime.

Friends Alternative Service in World War I

The American entry into the war in 1917 came as a surprise and within eighteen months it was over. The war inflicted its fury on the peace churches with an intensity for which they were completely unprepared. It enveloped them in ways none of them anticipated.

The pervasiveness of total war and the military draft

took on its characteristically draconian feature: total equality was enforced with all the unremitting power of the warfare state. In a few short months the military enlistment machinery cataloged and mobilized an entire generation of young Americans for military purposes. A few months later their elders felt the bite of the war bond, an ingenious device to finance the war effort.

The twin resources of modern warfare—manpower and money—were mobilized with swift thoroughness. For those conscientiously unable to cooperate, it was a fearful time.

British Friends responded to the war almost immediately. In August 1914 *The Friend* (London) carried a letter by Philip J. Boher, youthful Friend and authority in international law, calling on young men of the Society of Friends to form an ambulance unit of 48 persons to serve under the neutral auspices of the Red Cross. Boher believed the ambulance unit "would probably result in the saving of a great many lives, and in the alleviation of a great deal of suffering among the primary victims of war."

The Friends Ambulance Unit was created. The first party left English shores for the port of Dunkirk on October 31. Its first assignment was relief work in the wreckage wrought during the Battle of the Marne, September 6 to 9.

English and Irish Friends also reactivated the Friends War Victims Relief Committee. Collaborating in both these ventures was Rufus M. Jones, Professor of Philosophy at Haverford College and an authority on Quaker history and thought. Jones arranged for four young American Friends—Earl Fowler, Howard Carey, Edward Rice, and Felix Morley—to join the Ambulance Unit in France in

1915. Upon their return in 1916 they spoke to many audiences regarding their experiences.

Morley, later a Rhodes scholar and Pulitzer-prize editor, expressed his sense of urgency in the August 10 issue of *The Friend* (Philadelphia): "This war is very much our business. Starving folk cannot appreciate abstract sympathy." He cited the plight of English Friends struggling to support their relief program as the British economy sagged under the prolonged war. He pleaded that American Friends not fail them as they ministered to the wounded and the refugees and as they began the long slow reconstruction of the devastated French countryside.[7]

With the breaking of diplomatic relations with Germany in early 1917, American Friends began to reflect on an appropriate response to the mounting emergency. During a faculty meeting at Haverford College in early March, a committee of five was appointed "to consider the formation of a training unit of some sort, possibly an ambulance corps." The purpose of the Haverford Emergency Unit was "to provide a reasonable opportunity for Haverford men to prepare in unison for a national emergency without necessitating withdrawal from college work or the sacrifice of individual conscience."

On April 6, the day war was declared by Congress, the Haverford College Student Association voted 158 to 6 in favor of a training plan. A joint faculty-student meeting later in the day formally adopted a comprehensive training program in motor touring, shop work, Red Cross work, camping, hiking, and drill. Within a few weeks $10,000 was raised and a strenuous training schedule was launched.[8]

But the Emergency Unit faded as quickly as it had

formed. With commencement in May its members scattered. Its significance lay in the idea, for it served as a prelude to the Haverford Reconstruction Unit which formed in the summer, after conscription began in earnest and alternative forms of service became a high priority for absolute conscientious objectors.

American Friends Service Committee

The declaration of war and the introduction of a conscription bill in April precipitated a historic meeting of thirteen Friends on April 30, 1917. They met at the Friends meetinghouse at 15th and Race Streets in Philadelphia "to consider what might be appropriate Quaker action in the war emergency." The group represented a variety of American Friends.

Henry J. Cadbury, a professor at Haverford College, served as Clerk of the Meeting and recorded the following minute: "We are united in expressing our love for our country and our desire to serve her loyally. We offer our services to the government of the United States in any constructive work in which we can conscientiously serve humanity."[9]

With that was born the American Friends Service Committee. Rufus Jones was elected chairman; Alfred G. Scattergood, vice-chairman; Charles F. Jenkins, treasurer; and Vincent D. Nicholson, executive secretary, to handle the day-to-day details of the new organization. Headquarters were established in the historic Friends meetinghouse at 20 South 12th Street in Philadelphia.[10]

The founding of the American Friends Service Committee gave the Society of Friends (and subsequently others) an organization to work at two basic concerns which devolved on conscientious objectors in World War I: (1) securing exemption from military service, both combatant and noncombatant; (2) forging a program for alternative service satisfactory to a government at war and to consciences that could not support war.

In casting about for the means to do alternative service, several hopeful possibilities appeared. One was the appointment by President Wilson of Grayson Murphy as chief of the American Red Cross in France. Murphy was a graduate of the William Penn Charter School in Philadelphia and had been a student at Haverford College where he was on close terms with Rufus Jones.

Jones approached Murphy about a prospective Friends unit for relief work in France. The idea appealed to Murphy, and after a conference with the American Friends Service Committee, he suggested that a delegation of Friends visit France, confer with English Quakers there, and survey the needs. After receiving the blessing of Henry P. Davison, Wilson's new director of foreign relief work, J. Henry Scattergood and Morris Leeds left New York on June 2. They reached France before the first contingent of American troops. The reports of Scattergood and Leeds became the basis for the plans already under way for a reconstruction unit of American Friends in France.[11]

The training program for what came to be known as the Friends Reconstruction Unit began in early June. A committee screened candidates for service as applications streamed in. An intensive six-week course of study, work, and worship was designed, including physical conditioning, French language study, public sanitation, social service, first aid, carpentry, auto repair, and each evening, a time for silent gathered worship.

The reports of Scattergood and Leeds indicated that a desperate need for housing existed. Hence a model house was constructed to give trainees experience in construction. The last days at Haverford were spent in packing tools and medical and surgical equipment.

Hopes ran high. The American Friends Service Committee slogan, "A Service of Love in Wartime," seemed to be coming to fruition. During the hectic summer of 1917 it appeared that an alternative peace program was being constructed.[12] "As Friends we cannot bear arms against fellow men," wrote Walter C. Woodward in an editorial in the April 19 *American Friend.* "Neither are many of us clear to do service of any kind under the direct command of the military arm of the government. In our right, however, we can repair the waste places, relieve the suffering, bind up the wounds, and help bridge the chasm of hate which is the fruit of war."

But dedication and skills were not enough. America was in the tightening vise of total war. Factory, farm, railroad, post office, and store—all were being pressed into one gigantic war machine. Exceptions and exemptions were hard to come by. By late summer of 1917, Rufus Jones ruefully admitted, "We assumed, no doubt too hastily, that the President and exemption boards would gladly recognize that our reconstruction work abroad was a voluntary and unforced type of noncombatant service, entirely satisfactory for the fulfillment of the provisions."[13]

He could not have known that the centuries-long search by conscientious objectors for an alternative service in lieu of participation in war had not yet ended. The search and the struggle would have to continue.

CHAPTER 2

The Politics of Alternative Service in World War I

"Don't worry. We'll take care of your boys."
—Secretary of War Newton D. Baker
to D. D. Miller, 1917

March to War

When the war began in August 1914, Americans were secure in the conviction that it was not their concern. President Wilson declared that America "Neither sits in judgment upon others nor is disturbed in her own counsels." America would remain "neutral in fact as well as in name ... impartial in thought as well as in action." Americans saw the war as a case of European militarism run amok whose ultimate denouement would not affect the United States.

The *Lusitania* incident in May 1915 marked a turning point in American attitudes about the war. For the first time it became apparent that the U.S. could find itself drawn into the maelstrom. During the great debate over neutral rights in the summer of 1915, President Wilson came out for preparedness and the cabinet began drafting plans for rearmament. Preparedness, Wilson argued, was no longer a partisan cause, but a national necessity.

In January 1916 he toured the East and Midwest explaining and defending his preparedness program. But on his return to Washington on February 4 it was clear that Congress would reject the Continental Army plan proposed by Secretary of War Garrison. Garrison resigned. His replacement was Newton D. Baker, mayor of Cleveland. Popular with Congressional Democrats, he was an early supporter of preparedness. Wilson's preparedness program in Congress began to make steady progress.

The passage of the National Defense Act on June 2, 1916, enlarged the Military Academy, doubled the authorized peacetime strength of the regular army, integrated the National Guard into the national defense system, and established a program of volunteer summer military training camps.

It also introduced a selective draft option, known as the "Haydon Joker," buried in an obscure paragraph of the bill. Since any mention of a draft bill would have been anathema to a majority in Congress, the Congressional managers of the bill played down its presence. Only a few members of Congress knew of its existence. Wilson and Baker knew of the clause, but Wilson, with wonderful verisimilitude, argued that it applied only in time of war and was not really conscription, but a "draft in a more limited sense of the term."[1]

Wilson was reelected in November 1916 by a narrow margin after a campaign built around the slogan, "He kept us out of war." But events began to shorten the president's neutrality options. On January 3, 1917, Germany announced an unrestricted submarine warfare zone around the British Isles and the coast of Europe. In response, Wilson severed diplomatic relations with Germany on February 3.

The Draft Act

The next day, President Wilson suddenly appeared—unattended and unannounced—at Secretary of War Newton D. Baker's office for a conference. Upon his departure the secretary sent for General Crowder, his Judge Advocate General. The president, Baker informed Crowder, had decided upon a draft to recruit and augment the manpower of the regular army. He wanted a legislative draft proposal drawn up by 10:00 a.m. the next morning. Crowder, taken aback, inquired whether the president had expressed any opinion regarding the components of such a proposal. No, replied Baker, the war department would need to rely on its own resources.

At that moment, Crowder realized that his extracurricular interest in military manpower recruitment issues had not been in vain. Crowder had been trained at West Point and at the Law School of the University of Missouri. Years earlier, as a young cavalry officer stationed at a frontier army post, he had made an exhaustive study of the Civil War draft act and its administration.

The essential features of an improved draft law were already present in Crowder's well-organized mind. The law would ask for personal registration at a designated place rather than a house-to-house census. Draftees would be credited to their district of permanent residence. Quotas would be based on states rather than congressional districts. The use of bounties or the employment of substitutes would definitely be prohibited. Finally, one's service would be for the duration of the war. Furthermore, all male citizens of a designated age cohort must be enrolled.

Crowder sketched out his ideas in general form, identified the major elements of the proposal, and then asked each of his four assistants to work on a draft of a designated section. During the night refinements were made. Early on February 4, Crowder wrote out in almost final form the language subsequently submitted to Congress. A few minutes before 10:00 a.m. Crowder handed the prepared typescript to Secretary Baker. During the following weeks the document was further refined.

On April 6, the United States formally entered the war. The next day, April 7, the bill entitled "An Act to Authorize the President to Increase Temporarily the Military Establishment of the United States," was laid before the Congress by Secretary Baker.[2]

Conscription had many opponents in Congress. Hearings and debate consumed more than a month. It was not until May 18 that the Selective Training Act was finally signed into law by President Wilson. He hailed it as "In no sense a conscription of the unwilling; rather it is a selection from a nation which has volunteered en masse."[3] His rhetoric overlooked the fact that the Act he was signing into law made only cursory reference to those who for conscience' sake were unable to be conscripted.

The Act did have a conscientious objector provision:

Nothing in this act contained shall be construed or compel any person to serve in any of the forces herein provided for,

who is found to be a member of any well-recognized religious sect or organization at present organized and existing
and whose existing creed or principles forbid its members to
participate in war in any form and whose religious convictions are against war or participation therein in accordance
with the creed or principles of said religious organizations;
but no person so exempted shall be exempted from service
in any capacity that the President shall declare to be noncombatant.[4]

The conscientious objector clause presented a serious
problem for the peace churches. It provided no remedy for
absolutists who could not engage in noncombatant activity.
This limited its utility for peace church conscientious objectors although the phrase giving the president authority to
define noncombatancy was interpreted by the peace
churches as a means to meet their expectations and needs.
The delay in the first instance by the president to define
noncombatancy for a year—and then, when he finally
made his definition, defining it only in military terms—left
peace church conscientious objectors at the mercy of the
powerful, sometimes evasive, officials of the war department.

The Meaning of Noncombatancy

Even before the Selective Training Bill became law,
several groups attempted to effect changes. On April 12, a
week after Congress began its deliberations on the bill,
three Kansas Mennonites, P. H. Richert, Maxwell H.
Kratz, and Peter Jansen visited Washington to lobby for ex-
plicit exemption of the conscientious objector from military
service.[5]

That same day Lillian Wald, Jane Addams, and Norman Thomas made an eloquent plea to Secretary of War Baker to base conscientious objector exemption on an individual basis and to make clear provision for those conscientious objectors who could not accept noncombatant service.[6] The three spoke for the American Union Against Militarism, a prestigious anti-war group, which was soon to create the American Civil Liberties Union. Secretary Baker had once been a member of the AUAM. And Jane Addams, who was respected and admired by Wilson and Baker, sat on the executive committee of the AUAM. This led the group to believe their representation might have some effect.

Baker's noncommittal response gave faint hope, however, and as debate continued on the bill in Congress, Norman Thomas wrote a letter to General Crowder and to Senator Chamberlain, chairman of the Senate Military Affairs Committee, urging that "an alternative service of recognized value to the state" be created for those unable to do noncombatant service.[7]

Jane Addams followed Thomas' letter with a strongly worded telegram to Baker requesting that the AUAM concerns presented on April 12 be taken seriously.[8] Baker replied:

> Your telegram of the 27th reached me. I think it is unlikely that we can secure a legislative exemption for conscientious objectors. I will, however, see that your view is presented to the Conference Committee. In the meantime I hope that the Administration of whatever law is passed will make it possible for us to avoid the unhappy difficulties which occured in England and which you mention.[9]

Roger Baldwin of the new American Civil Liberties Union wrote to the Senate and House Committee urging especially the recognition of conscientious objectors who were not members of a "well-recognized sect opposed to war."[10]

Baker and Crowder gave three days' testimony before the House and Senate Military Committees. At one point they were closely questioned by Congressman Anthony who objected to any exemptions—religious or otherwise. Baker stoutly responded, "It is a part of the policy of the government to allow liberty of conscience, and where men are actually members of religious bodies which have entertained that view, they have never been required in this country to fight."

But, persisted Anthony, are members of religious groups totally exempted?

Replied General Crowder, "That is right. Here the exemption is complete for religious people."

Then, in a fateful exchange that proved to be a foretaste of things to come, the Congressman observed, "It occurs to me that as the class of men you propose to draft under this bill are to be from 19 to 24, and all active men, their religious beliefs must be rather immature, and would it not really be better to give them service in the noncombatant corps?"

"I have no objection to that," replied Baker.[11]

Both Wilson and Baker, from the outset, had taken a firm stand against individual conscientious exemption. Wilson insisted it would be "impossible ... because it would open the door to so much that was unconscientious on the part of persons who wished to escape service."[12]

Baker was aware of the abuses of exemptions in the Civil

War. Thus he observed to Wilson that "so many kinds of people have asked for class exemptions that our only safety seems to be in making none."[13] Congress apparently agreed, for when Senator Robert LaFollette and Representative Edward Keating offered an amendment recognizing political conscientious objectors, it was supported by only a few of their colleagues. Congress and the war department were afraid of anything which would encourage "slackers and draft dodgers."[14]

June 5, 1917, was registration day. Wilson hailed it as a "great day of patriotic devotion and obligation."[15] For the peace churches it was another step toward the drafting of their young men. Furthermore, the pressure of the war spirit was beginning to make itself felt. Wilson led the charge with a Flag Day speech in which he called the peace movement one of traitors and schemers. The next day Congress passed the Espionage Act.[16] Summer 1917 was a time of anxiety for the peace churches, as they sought to bring their concerns to the attention of the war department.

A number of peace church leaders felt a strong need to organize a common effort to deal with the war department. A few days after the passage of the Draft Act, six representatives of the peace churches met in Washington, D.C., to explore common action. Their call for a "committee which, in a united and concerted way, may have watch over the situation, devise plans, present our position and claims to the various departments of our government, and labor together in the interests of our time-honored and Scriptural teachings of peace" appears in retrospect as a timely and important initiative. But it was never effected in the course of the war.[17] The absence of such a unified effort contributed to the difficulties encountered by peace church conscientious objectors in World War I.

The lack of a strong concerted peace church lobby did not mean an absence of effort. On the contrary, a constant stream of delegations visited Washington from all the peace groups. They found surprisingly quick and easy access to Secretary Baker, Judge Advocate General Crowder, and others at the war department. In fact, it is difficult to believe that more activity could have been useful. The problem was not representation and presence. Secretary Baker was bombarded by peace church concerns. Rather, the unorganized and episodic character of the initiatives gave Baker freedom to maneuver around the appeals. Indeed, he skillfully used the situation, cajoling and shifting ground as he met delegation after delegation.

Baker sought to be reassuring. When the newly created Mennonite War Problems Committee—Aaron Loucks, D. D. Miller, and S. G. Shetler—visited him in late summer he concluded the interview by affably putting his hand on D. D. Miller's knee with the words, "Don't worry. We'll take care of your boys." [18]

Baker insisted that the deficiencies in the legislation would be remedied by administrative process, but refused to actually define how that process would occur. General Crowder, brusque and genuinely unsympathetic to conscientious objectors, played a tough role. The churchmen were continually thrown off balance by his hard-line interpretations of policy, although he probably represented the true line of policy more accurately than his superior, Secretary Baker.

The failure of the peace churches to unite their efforts was largely due to the decentralized character of the church organizations and a genuine confusion among the groups about what constituted appropriate noncombatant behavior. The immobilization resulting from an inability to get consensus on the issue of how far to cooperate was graphically portrayed by C. E. Boyers, who represented the Church of the Brethren at Camp Meade. Reported Boyers:

> Only last week the captain said he needed men in the Medical Corps badly and asked whether our church would oppose work there. Finally, I ventured to say I thought they would not. He asked if I would put that in writing. I replied that I had no authority to speak for the church. You see? Would appreciate a word on this point.[19]

From Camp Funston came the plaintive, "We don't know how far to go because our church hasn't defined our privilege."[20]

For peace church leaders, the ability to answer such queries was linked to what could be hoped for by way of war department policy. All of the peace churches sought total exemption as an ideal. Only the more conservative Mennonites were prepared to insist on that stance for all of their young men. The Brethren and Friends were less directive, giving their young men freedom of choice.

The uncertainties felt by peace church leaders during the summer of 1917 were heightened by two policy statements in August by the war department. A ruling on August 8 for the first time stated in unmistakable language that all draftees are "in the military service of the United States from the time specified for reporting to the Local Board for military service."[21] The peace churches had hoped to avoid becoming part of the military apparatus.

The second ruling, on August 11, was equally discon-
certing. All designated conscientious objector draftees
would be "forwarded to a mobilization camp" and treated
as part of the draft quota of a state and district.[22]
Conscientious objectors were to be physically placed in
Army camps, a development viewed with alarm by all the
peace churches.

During the discussions following these rulings a forceful
advocate for the peace churches came forward in the
person of W. W. Griest, Congressman from Lancaster,
Pennsylvania, whose district included large populations of
Friends, Mennonites, and Brethren. Griest was a Quaker,
minority leader of the Agriculture Committee in the House
of Representatives, and genuinely interested in the rights
of his peace church constituents. He not only opened doors
for peace church representatives in Washington, but actively worked on their behalf.

Thus in July, even before the war department rulings, he
had written to Wilson and Crowder requesting agricultural
deferments for Mennonites, acting on a request from the
Lancaster Mennonite Conference Bishop Board.[23] After
the August war department rulings, Griest wrote an eloquent and strongly worded letter to President Wilson:

> Living in the midst of the nonresistant religious sects of
> Southeastern Pennsylvania—the Dunkards, the Amish, the
> Quakers, and the Mennonites—I wish to direct your atten-
> tion to the unrest and alarm recently aroused among them
> by your regulations which they think will deprive them of
> the considerations accorded their religions by the Selective
> Draft Act.[24]

Why were they so alarmed?

To be posted as selected for military service on Form 164, to
be assembled and sent to mobilization camp as one selected
for military service; probably to be dealt with there either as
a menial or arrayed in uniform which is a dress contrary to
his religious beliefs and principles and the Creed of his
church, and to be treated in all respects as one selected for
military service except for the certificate he holds and which
the government will have no record of, is according to these
plain, but loyal folk a lack of consideration which would appear to be unnecessary and in contravention of the spirit of
the Selective Draft Law, and contrary to all draft measures
ever enacted in this country from colonial days down to the
present time, during all the wars of American history.[25]

Griest also urgently encouraged the peace churches to
send delegations to Baker and the war department. "The
most important thing," he told W. J. Swigart of the
Brethren Peace Committee, "is to reverse the order by
Crowder that conscientious objector registrants be consigned at once to military encampments."[26]

The peace church leaders responded with alacrity. On
August 17 the American Friends Service Committee com-
missioned Isaac Sharpless and Henry Bartlett to see Baker
about the matter. They did so on August 22. Baker was cor-
dial but tough.

"Would hospital service be agreeable to Quakers?" he
asked.

"Not generally," was the reply. "How will Friends be
treated when they get to camp?" the Friends inquired.

"They will be given the hospital option. If they refuse,
they will be locked in the Guard House and court-
martialed," replied Baker.

"Why not exempt conscientious objectors for service with the Friends Reconstruction Unit and avoid such troubles?" the Friends asked.

"That can't be considered because it would generate too many conscientious objector exemption cases," Baker replied.

"Would it help to see Wilson?"

"No," replied Baker, "but I will see that Wilson receives your letter of concern."

As usual Baker's anteroom was crowded with persons waiting to see him and so he quickly ushered the Friends into the next office to see Crowder. The latter was taciturn and dour.

"I wrote the act," he said. "It is a military measure. Where the word *service* is used it means military service."

"What," the Friends asked, "would happen if Friends refused all service?"

"I'm sorry you asked that, for it would not be pleasant for you to know or for me to contemplate." Sharpless and Bartless assumed he meant the men would be shot.[27]

Two days later, on August 25, four Hutterites from South Dakota visited Baker, and were assured that "the best will be done" for them. Their young men, Baker said, would "not be compelled to do that which is contrary to the dictates of their conscience."

The editor of the Mennonite *Gospel Herald* was relieved. "This is indeed good news to us whose positions on the question of military service is the same as theirs."[28]

On August 28 a delegation of Friends, led by Rufus Jones, presented an eloquent proposal to Baker. The war department rulings created, as they put it, " 'a very grave situation.' You have a problem. Many of our young men will not be able to cooperate with your definitions of non-combatancy. We can help you solve the problem by having the American Friends Service committee find 'service of national importance' for all Friends who are conscientious objectors." Under the provisions of the draft regulations, the Committee argued, the president may discharge conscientious objectors, and "this Committee pledges itself to find forms of service to be approved by the President for all such men." They pointed to the success of such a plan in Britain and New Zealand and the precedents established during the American Civil War.[29]

On September 1 two delegations visited Baker. An eight-man Mennonite group reported on the Mennonite position, just redefined at a conference at Goshen, Indiana, a few days earlier. One member of the group, A. G. Clemmer, had the foresight to quickly summarize the main lines of the discussion with Baker. He cited ten provisions the secretary promised to follow.[30]

Later that same day W. J. Swigart, I. W. Taylor, and W. M. Lyon of the Church of the Brethren carried Clemmer's summary into an interview with Baker. Baker was surprised by the document, but after a careful perusal agreed to its essential accuracy, taking exception only with item 8, the key issue at hand.

"It would not be possible," he said, "to say finally, 'Those who accept noncombatant service will be assigned to some other service not under the military arm of the government.' It may possibly be so, but that would have to be worked out."

To the dismay of the churchmen he went on to say, "And on the absolute refusal to obey orders and accept assignments from officers in charge, some might be imprisoned for a time. But provisions will be made for adjustment. Go as far as you can, and all claims for conscience will be heard."[31]

Thus after a series of five visits by peace church delegations within a period of one week, Baker was still unwilling to concede the most important point: that peace church conscientious objectors be freed from military control. Nor did he respond to peace church proposals for alternative service. In the midst of this intense lobbying, Baker revealed his real intentions in a letter to President Wilson:

> It does not seem to me that it would be wise now to designate this work of reconstruction as the sort of noncombatant service contemplated for religious objectors, chiefly for the reasons that any definition of that sort of work at this time may have the effect of encouraging further "conscientious objecting." On this whole subject my belief is that we ought to proceed with the draft, and after the conscientious objectors have gotten into the camps and have made known their inability to proceed with military work, their number will be ascertained and a suitable work evolved for them.[32]

The Remedy for Noncombatancy

The first wave of draftees, aged 21 to 31, began to arrive at the training camps on September 5. The inability of the peace churches to gain war department action on the conscientious objector issue now meant that the burden of what constituted appropriate behavior—where to draw the line in terms of cooperation in the training camps—fell swiftly and forcefully on the shoulders of the young conscientious objector draftees themselves. The war department immediately began to take advantage of this situation.

In late September 1917, Secretary Baker visited Camp Meade in Maryland to inspect an "interesting group of conscientious objectors."[33] Out of that visit evolved a strategy he hoped would persuade conscientious objectors to cooperate with the government. His policy, he informed President Wilson, was to segregate the conscientious objectors from their fellow soldiers. The feeling of rejection, he was sure, would soon bring them around to cooperation and only a hard core of Amish, Quakers, and Fundamentalists would be left.[34]

In October he issued orders that conscientious objectors should be separated from military personnel, treated with tact and consideration, and unless they refused a lawful order, they should not be court-martialed.[35] But the army soon made a shambles of Baker's intentions. Court-martials handing down 25-year sentences became commonplace. Physical abuse became rampant. Clarifying orders by the war department on handling conscientious objectors did not improve matters.

The problem lay, of course, in the absence of a clear policy and the fact that the officers in charge were almost never in sympathy with such policy as existed. The powerful public propaganda machine, designed to mobilize support for the war effort, combined with the formalized military legal machinery, placed conscientious objectors in a perilous position. Their religious convictions and civil rights counted for little. Baker and the war department were intent on keeping the number of conscientious objectors who persevered as few as possible—even at the price of an abridgment of civil liberties.

As autumn became winter the plight of young conscientious objectors caught in the web of a military system geared to wean them from their conscientious objector convictions became ever more difficult. Peace church leaders struggled to create a network of support to help mitigate some of the worst cases of mishandling and abuse. The war department became increasingly unresponsive to the plight of conscientious objectors as the weight of the war effort began to strain the available economic, transport, and personnel systems. Until some definitive resolution could be made to remand conscientious objectors to useful civilian pursuits, the dilemma of the conscientious objectors would continue to worsen. The peace churches sought to pressure the president to declare what constituted noncombatancy, but given his and Baker's intentions vis-à-vis the conscientious objector problem, it was not surprising that they were not inclined to move on a definition.

The conscientious objector problem would not go away, however. Finally, on January 8, 1918, Baker addressed a letter to Senator Chamberlain of the Senate Military Affairs Committee:

> I enclose herewith for the consideration and appropriate action of the Senate Military Committee, a joint resolution authorizing the Secretary of War to grant furloughs to enlisted men of the army with or without pay and allowances, to permit said enlisted men to engage in civil occupations and pursuits.
>
> The main purpose for which it is intended to use this authority is to furlough soldiers in the National Army during harvest and planting time to enable them to assist the agricultural production of the country.

Under the law as it now stands the furloughed men would be entitled to pay and allowances during the period of their absence. It is necessary, therefore, to have authority to grant such furloughs without raising a claim against the Government for pay.[36]

Clearly the Wilson administration was reaching for a resolution of the conscientious objector problem. President Wilson confirmed this in a letter to H. C. Early, moderator of the Church of the Brethren, on February 12.

The Secretary of War has presented to the Congress for approval, a bill which will authorize the War Department to furlough, without pay, men in the military service. Should the Congress enact this legislation, it will then be possible under its provision, to assign, by conditional furlough, men whose conscientious scruples cannot otherwise be met, to civilian occupations of the general sort of which you indicate.[37]

The Furlough Act was passed on March 16. A few days later, Rufus Jones, reporting on yet another trip to the war department, observed that the new act gave the secretary of war authority to furlough conscientious objectors for civilian work. Thus, he remarked, the president won't need to rule on what constituted appropriate noncombatant work for conscientious objectors.[38]

However, almost as Jones was speaking, the president did rule on appropriate noncombatant work. On March 20 he issued executive order 2823. As the American Friends Service Peace Committee noted, this order made the conscientious objector position even more tenuous. Now conscientious objectors refusing any of the options became subject to punishment for refusing such service.[39]

The administration, however, had cleverly managed to find a way to move conscientious objectors quietly into civilian service while preserving the guise of being tough on conscientious objectors. By not recognizing a civilian alternative in his March 20 order, Wilson preserved himself from criticism for being "soft" on conscientious objectors. This was admittedly a serious problem, largely generated by the powerful war propaganda campaign under way. For the president to have reflected sympathy for the conscientious objector in the spring of 1918 would have been politically inexpedient.

In any case the American Friends Service Peace Committee accurately diagnosed the meaning of these events. Rufus Jones, Stanly Yarnall, and Vincent Nicholson immediately visited the war department. Baker was absent in France but Baker's secretary, Dr. Frederick Keppel, agreed that the Furlough Act did provide a loophole for furloughing conscientious objectors to civilian work. Keppel went on to suggest that the Mennonites, Brethren, and Friends should form a joint commission to organize and give direction to the young men released by the Furlough Act.[40]

Jones acted swiftly. On April 4 a conference of peace church leaders convened in Philadelphia and created a joint commission, composed of nine men of "broad and understanding sympathies," three from each of the peace churches. The commission would be responsible to arrange employment for and give oversight to the men furloughed by the war department. The commission would place men in civilian employ on a priority basis—first to agriculture; second, reconstruction and relief abroad; third, forestry;

and finally, such other general civilian work as could be agreed upon by the commission and the war department. The commission would be committed to make periodic reports to the war department regarding the status of each man in its charge.[41]

Frederick Keppel, third assistant secretary of war, formerly dean of Columbia University, became the key war department official in the development of the plan to solve the conscientious objector problem. However, resolution of the issue continued to founder on the desire of the war department to appear tough on the conscientious objector. The department no longer feared large-scale conscientious objector defections. The war department, as reported by the *New York Times*, was at pains to note that as of June 1, 1918, only 600 bona fide conscientious objectors had emerged out of a total of 1,300,000 men drafted. Furthermore, as the article noted, the war department hoped the newly created Board of Inquiry would reduce the numbers even more.[42]

At issue now was simply the need to avoid all appearance of special privilege for conscientious objectors given the temper of public opinion. Having found a device to legally furlough conscientious objectors, the problem now was to design a means—a test—to determine sincerity. Keppel found the answer in a Board of Inquiry.

On May 31 Rufus Jones reported to Professor Swigart of the Church of the Brethren that he had just met with Keppel who assured him that the plan for furloughing conscientious objectors was "practically perfected, with a few alterations." Keppel was sure the secretary of war would agree with the plan and announce it in a very short time.

Jones acknowledged that "this proposed plan is by no means what we want. It is, however, almost certainly the best we can get through the war department." Jones went on to observe that

> it is the settled judgment in Washington that the so-called exemption clause in the draft law never looked toward the exemption of our conscientious objectors from noncombatant service. It apparently did not occur to the Washington people that our objection was anything more than an objection to the direct killing of people. They do not seem to understand that we are opposed to the military system and all forms of service under such a system. I find it difficult to make anybody in Washington realize that attitude.[43]

The war department announced the new plan for handling absolute conscientious objectors on May 30. All conscientious objectors were to be moved to Fort Leavenworth, Kansas. A Board of Inquiry, chaired by Major Richard C. Stoddert of the judge advocate's office (later Walter C. Kellogg replaced Stoddert), was created. The other members were Judge Julian W. Mack of the federal court and Dean Harlan F. Stone of Columbia University Law School.

Absolute conscientious objectors were to be furloughed without pay for agricultural service. If the farmer provided compensation, it was to be at the compensation level of a private. In exceptional cases the Board of Inquiry could furlough men for service in France with the Friends Reconstruction Unit. All conscientious objectors recommended for furloughs had to accept it.

Finally, to the dismay of peace church leaders the directive decreed that in no case could the furloughed men escape their military status. All military regulations remained in effect.[44]

Rufus Jones was again dispatched to Washington by the executive committee of the American Friends Service Committee. Once the sincerity of the conscientious objector was validated, who would the men be remanded to, he inquired of Keppel. Keppel identified three possibilities: the United States Department of Agriculture, local draft boards of the respective men, or the peace church joint commission. Jones urged the latter.

The war department was uneasy about that idea, however, and proposed a military commissioner. As Jones later acknowledged, the peace church commission was "sure to be open to criticism on the part of those who wanted severe measures used toward these men, and persons of such attitude could hardly approve of turning the conscientious objectors over to the tender mercies of their own friends and people."

Jones, trading on his good relations with Keppel, was able to modify the appointment to be a civilian commissioner, who, as he put it, "understands the conscientious objector point of view." Jones acknowledged that the joint commission will "not have any large amount of work to do," but would serve as counsel to the commissioner.[45]

Unfortunately Keppel's optimistic hopes of finding a civilian commissioner "in a few days" lapsed into a few months. It was not until August 3 that he informed the peace churches of the appointment of Dr. Roswell N. McCrea of the Columbia University School of Business as the new commissioner. McCrea was a graduate of Haverford College and understood the peace church perspective on war. But by then the war was almost over and the work of the commission never really got under way,[46]

No solution was found during World War I which dealt adequately with the problem of the absolute conscientious objector. The war department plan to place young conscientious objectors in military camps to test their sincerity—and, if possible, convince them to accept some form of military or noncombatant service—was clearly unsatisfactory. But the logic of the warfare state with its all-consuming need to bring everything and everyone into the orbit of the war effort, created nearly insurmountable obstacles to nonmilitary alternatives for those who could not participate.

The solution for conscientious objectors clearly lay in the design of a civilian alternative to military service. The Farm Furlough Act, passed by an unsuspecting Congress and administered with gingerly reticence by the war department, did not resolve the issue, for it failed to free the absolute conscientious objector from the tentacles of the military machine. The only resolution with promise was seconding conscientious objectors to the Friends Reconstruction Units in France. But this process became possible only late in the war, and was able to absorb only a limited percentage of conscientious objectors.

The failure to achieve a satisfactory resolution for the absolute objector was not a result of an absence of effort by the historic peace churches. A better coordinated effort might have helped, but given the obdurant posture of the war department, it is doubtful that even a united front would have accomplished more. Not having waged a conscript war for more than fifty years, the war department was unprepared for the tenacious convictions of conscripted conscientious objectors. By the time they realized their mistake, the war was over.

World War I was a searing experience for the historic peace churches. The memory of that experience was to bulk large in the search for an early resolution of the problem at the onset of World War II. The general shape and form taken by Civilian Public Service in World War II was a product of the failure of the war department and the peace churches to develop a viable policy in World War I.

CHAPTER 3

The Historic Peace Church Quest For Alternative Service Models

"If in a future war there is any provision for exemption from military service it will probably be due to the fact that the nonresistant people themselves devised the plan."
—Mennonite Guy F. Hershberger, 1935

Response to War

The return of peace church conscientious objectors to their communities in 1919 was a time of celebration, but it also heightened awareness that what had transpired during the war could readily be repeated.

Ominously, numerous bills promoting universal military training were submitted to Congress during 1919. Most called for all young men between the ages of 18 and 26 to undergo a two-year course of training. After training, they would become members of a national reserve.

The specter of wartime conscription now transformed into peacetime conscription generated enormous concern among the peace churches.[1] Church of the Brethren Moderator H. C. Early claimed that the enactment of universal military training would "not be less than a calamity." He urged W. J. Swigart, chairman of the Brethren peace committee, to be aggressive in opposition. Early led his Virginia district committee in drafting an uncharacteristically strong protest statement.[2]

The often quietistic Mennonites launched an aggressive petition campaign which garnered 20,000 Mennonite signatures (one in four Mennonites in 1919) protesting passage of peacetime conscription and asking for conscientious objector exemption.[3] The Friends were equally concerned and active.

Each of the groups turned to assess their wartime experience. The Friends found a great vehicle in the elaborate reports they prepared for the Conference of All Friends, a world conference held in London in August 1920. Seven commissions addressed various aspects of the recent war in light of Friends peace concerns.

Commission VII somewhat critically observed:

> It is, perhaps, to the discredit of American Friends, that it required the entry of the United States into the war to produce a sense of obligation for service in the world emergency.... The international service of American Friends during the war was closely interwoven from the first with the conscription law.... This fact should be borne in mind in considering the possibilities of somewhat similar work in the future.[4]

The Commission noted the creation of a subcommittee of the American Friends Service Committee, known as the Committee on Home Service Work, whose objective was to provide a year of work of national importance for young people in a variety of settings. The intention was to create a corps of young persons conversant with social, economic, and political problems and committed to the ideals of service. The idea grew out of the Friends reconstruction work during the war and the salutary effect that experience had on the young participants.

Commission V lamented the large number of Friends who opted for military noncombatant service, and stressed the need to be more resourceful in educating Friends for conscientious objection to noncombatancy and to the creation of opportunities for service in nonmilitary context.[5] Commission IV observed that "this is the practical problem when dealing with youth; to propose for bearing of arms some substitute which will make equal demands." Such service, the Commission believed, "would probably continue to be recognized by any administration in America as the equivalent of military service.[6]

Each of the historic peace churches established ongoing committees to pursue peace work and peace study. The Mennonites created a five-person Peace Problems Committee in 1919. In 1927 that committee assigned itself three major tasks: educate Mennonites in peace concerns, interpret nonresistance to others, and maintain contact with the government on peace-related issues.[7] The General Conference Mennonites appointed a Peace Committee in 1916.[8]

The war to make the world safe for democracy left massive desolation in its wake. While the world's government leaders struggled with political reconstruction, the peace churches turned their efforts to relief work. The American Friends Service Committee increased the scope of its French reconstruction work and both Mennonite and Brethren young men joined the work in France. The Friends work was not only an imaginative program of service to war sufferers; during the interwar period, it became a symbol of peace church idealism and a model for peace church thinking about alternative service.

Alternative Service Models

Actually, three models of alternative service were particularly instructive for the historic peace churches during the interwar period. One was the American Friends Service Committee program. A second was the work camp movement initiated by the Swiss pacifist Pierre Ceresole. The third was the Mennonite forestry service in Russia.

The Mennonite Forestry Service in Russia began in 1881 with the opening of two camps for 123 young conscientious objectors.[9] The camps were the result of a decade of negotiation between the Mennonites and the Russian government following the introduction of a conscription bill in 1870 which required all Russian citizens without exception to personally serve in the military. The conscription law had canceled a hundred years of Mennonite exemption from military service, first secured when the Mennonites were invited to settle in Russia in the eighteenth century. The exemption was renewed in 1800 and again in 1838. In the 1870s, the winds of nationalism swept through eastern Europe and compulsory universal service became one of its salient features.

The Russian government in the 1870s, like the American government in World War I, was quite ready to offer non-combatant service as an alternative to combatant service. What the government only slowly understood and reluctantly acknowledged was the Mennonite insistence on service under civilian auspices and for nonmilitary purposes. It was only the large-scale emigration of Mennonites to the United States and Canada which finally convinced the Russian government, loath to lose its best farmers, that an accommodation was necessary. The result was an alternative service, the Mennonite Forestry Service.

The task of the Mennonite Forestry Service was reforestation in South Russia. Length of service was identical to military service. The men were assigned to base camps where spiritual nurture could be provided. The Mennonites paid for the construction of the barracks which housed the men as well as for food and clothing. The government paid the men a nominal per diem.

The work of the men was under the supervision of the head forester in each district. The Mennonites administered their part of the program through a special Mennonite Forestry Service council which employed a Mennonite executive.

Funding the program was a major challenge. By World War I the program cost the Mennonites more than a quarter million dollars per year. During the war the cost grew dramatically as the number of conscientious objectors increased. A voluntary tax assessment levied by the Mennonite Forestry Service Council was the primary source of funds.

During the thirty-three years prior to 1914, the Mennonite Forestry Service served as a reasonably satisfactory alternative service. But the onset of World War I soon led to modifications. Within a short time nearly half of all Mennonite conscientious objectors had become noncombatants, the majority working in the Sanitary Service which operated military hospitals, ambulance trains, and medical services behind the front lines.

The Friends reconstruction work in France during and immediately after the war was an important model for alternative service. Despite many difficulties the American Friends Service Committee managed to place several hundred workers in France beginning in the fall of 1917. The work was carried on under the auspices of the American Red Cross in close cooperation with the British Friends. Some of the young men in its service were deferred draftees.

After the farm furlough program was implemented, a substantial number of conscientious objectors were sent to the Friends reconstruction units. As the peace churches discussed alternative service, the reconstruction units provided a helpful model.

The strength of the reconstruction program was the opportunity to be in close proximity to and deal with the actual consequences of the war itself. Rebuilding war-devastated housing, rehabilitating agriculture, providing medical and physical relief to civilian war sufferers—it was a perfect alternative, a form of sacrificial direct service which could hardly be improved upon. The chief drawback lay in its dependence on the Red Cross which during the late summer of 1917 was formally brought under the control of the war department. However the Red Cross provided essential logistical and financial support without which the program could hardly have been carried out.[10]

An important spin-off of the wartime Friends reconstruction work was the work camp movement. Pierre Ceresole—a Swiss engineer, convinced Quaker, and ardent pacifist—was greatly impressed by the Friends work in France. Having served time in Swiss prisons for his pacifist convictions, he was searching for some form of service which pacifists could perform as an alternative to military service.

In 1920 he broached the work camp idea in a speech to the Congress of the International Fellowship of Reconciliation in the Netherlands. His ideas caught on quickly. Soon a group of German and French young people were rebuilding devastated areas of northern France. The Service Civil Internationale spread throughout Europe under the direction of the Fellowship of Reconciliation, Friends, and other pacifists. It is estimated that more than 300,000 German young people—not to mention other nationalities—participated in the work camp movement during the 1920s.[11]

The key objective of the movement was to bring young people together in work—usually of a physical nature with humanitarian benefits. But it also provided a setting for young people from many walks of life to talk about the great issues of war, peace, and justice. The combination of altruistic work and constructive dialogue had significant effects on the young people involved.

Historic Peace Church Conferences

The tentative relationships created during the world war provided a context for the peace churches to work together during the interwar period. The first conference of peace churches at Bluffton College in Ohio in August 1923 was attended by a number of alumni of the Friends reconstruction units in France. Wilbur K. Thomas, the executive director of the American Friends Service Committee, was the featured speaker.

Out of the meeting came a new organization called the Conference of Pacifist Churches. This group sponsored a second meeting in 1925 at Wichita, Kansas, attended not only by peace church people, but by peace organization people, such as Frederick Libby of the National Council for Prevention of War, and Charles Clayton Morrison, editor of the *Christian Century* magazine.

Thereafter the Conference of Pacifist Churches held meetings at Carlock, Illinois, in 1926; at Manchester College in 1927; at Bethany Biblical Seminary in Chicago in 1928; and at Wilmington College in 1929. The last of the series was held at Mt. Morris, Illinois, in March 1931. There H. P. Krehbiel from Newton, Kansas, gave an address, "What Is a Pacifist?" which led to animated discussion and the appointment of Krehbiel, a Newton, Kansas, Mennonite, as a continuation committee of one to arrange the next conference.[12]

The death of Krehbiel's wife along with the disarray of the Great Depression and some Mennonite foot-dragging kept Krehbiel from carrying out his mandate until 1935. In early 1935 Krehbiel pressed ahead with plans for a conference.

Ominous signs abroad portended war. Hitler promulgated the Nurnburg Laws and repudiated the Versailles Treaty. Mussolini invaded Ethiopia. Japan was about to continue its invasion of North China. The dictators were on the march. The international scene lent urgency to Krehbiel's call for a conference.

However, the three peace churches had not been idle. Dan West, the tireless youth worker for the Church of the Brethren, began a "One Hundred Dunkers for Peace" movement which by 1935 had become "Two Hundred Thousand Dunkers for Peace."[13] In 1934 the Church of the Brethren made the Manchester College faculty its commission on peace. That year the annual conference urged its members to protest and oppose war taxes. In 1935 the annual conference drafted a statement which declared "all war is sin" and delivered the statement to President Roosevelt and Secretary of State Hull.[14]

Meanwhile, the Mennonite Peace Problems Committee under the leadership of E. L. Frey of Archbold, Ohio, drafted a disarmament statement. This statement was originally sent to the London Naval Conference in 1930. In 1933 the committee sent the statement in a cablegram to the Geneva Disarmament Conference: "In the name of 50,000 Mennonites whose historical Biblical position against war is known we urge utmost disarmament praying that [the Geneva Disarmament] conference accomplishes definite progress toward lasting peace."[15]

Orie Miller, secretary of the Peace Problems Committee, reported on the work of the committee to Mennonite General Conference in 1933. He urged preparation for constructive work in case of war. He reminded the conference that the church might not have lost so many men to the military had it been better prepared in 1917. Mennonites, he said, had also been "too much dependent on the Quakers."[16]

In planning for the conference, Krehbiel consulted with his own Western District Conference Peace Committee, and then approached C. Ray Keim—on the faculty of

Manchester College—for advice from the Brethren. Keim then contacted Robert W. Balderston of the Society of Friends, who lived in Chicago. Others—including Orie Miller of the Mennonite Peace Problems Committee, Richard R. Wood, executive secretary of the Friends Peace Committee of the Philadelphia Yearly Meetings, and Dan West of the Brethren—also participated in the planning.[17]

Krehbiel drafted a paper that focused on Jesus as peacemaker, entitled "Basis for an Ecumenical Conference of Historic Peace Churches in North America." The piece managed to steer clear of both Mennonite and Friends particulars, though Orie Miller, aware of vigilant fundamentalist Mennonite concerns, observed that deletion of the word *political* from the text would be desirable. Richard Wood felt it was too creedal. Robert Balderston would have liked to have more emphasis on the practical dimensions of peacemaking.[18]

The conference convened on October 31. For three days the fifty-seven delegates and twenty-two visitors engaged in worship, shared information with each other about their peace activities, and sought for common ground from which to move ahead together.[19] The result was an eight-point theological statement, a definition of patriotism in the peace church context, the creation of a joint committee of the historic peace churches, a procedure for the exchange of literature, and a plan of action in case of war.[20]

The importance of the conference lies in the genuine degree of consensus which was found among the groups despite the clear differences because so many of the major leaders of the peace efforts in subsequent years were present—many of them learning to know each other for the first time during those days.

Historic Peace Church Collaboration

The call by the conference for a joint committee of three persons appointed by Mennonite Central Committee, the Peace Committee of the Church of the Brethren, and the American Friends Service Committee was quickly heeded. Robert Balderston for the Friends, C. Ray Keim for the Brethren, and Orie Miller for the Mennonites began their responsibilities as a committee with a first meeting in Chicago on February 18, 1936. Among others attending were M. R. Zigler of the Brethren, who would play a large role in subsequent alternative service planning. Ray Wilson of the American Friends Service Committee, another pioneer in the World War II alternative service work, also attended. Among the issues addressed in the meeting were cooperative ventures in peace literature, conferencing, government contacts, and inevitably, finances.[21]

Of the three groups, the Mennonites (Old Mennonites) found the joint venture most problematical. Orie Miller, the Mennonite representative, had to proceed very carefully, lest the more conservative among the Mennonites would take exception to the relationship. Membership on the joint committee was made a Mennonite Central Committee assignment. It thus included General Conference Mennonites, Mennonite Brethren, and a number of other Mennonite groups more ready for historic peace church collaboration. The Mennonite connection was thus tenuously sustained, but the range of cooperation was clearly quite limited until 1939.[22]

The Brethren, on the other hand, began several important cooperative ventures with the Friends. In 1936 the American Friends Service Committee became a key organization in the nationwide Emergency Peace Campaign.

The focus of the campaign was to promote neutrality by the United States in any impending war. Ray Newton of the American Friends Service Committee was its chief executive.[23] Dan West, Brethren youth leader, was loaned to the Emergency Peace Campaign for a year by the Brethren Board of Christian Education. Roger Sappington comments that this cooperative work was one of the most comprehensive the Brethren had ever undertaken.[24]

Meanwhile, the American Friends Service Committee began relief work in Spain. In December 1936 Clarence Pickett, executive secretary of the American Friends Service Committee, inquired of M. R. Zigler whether the Church of the Brethren would like to assist.[25] Zigler was eager to be of help. Soon the indefatigable Dan West, along with fellow Brethren Martha Remple, David Blickenstaff, and Paul Bowman, Jr., were in Spain working with American Friends Service Committee people. A historic peace churches committee on Spain was set up and Mrs. Ross Murphy, a prominent Brethren leader from Philadelphia, represented the Brethren on the committee.[26]

The Brethren-Friends collaboration in the Spanish relief work offered evidence that historic peace church cooperation could be fruitful and desirable. John Reich, American Friends Service Committee secretary for the Spanish relief project, wanted the Brethren to understand how much Friends appreciated the shared work.

> We feel that the project in Spain has been most helpful in bringing together the three Historic Peace Churches in a practical service which gives us opportunities to understand each other and learn to work together. There may be great need for this in the future. We have always talked of our

unity. It is a satisfaction to us actually to achieve it through a common work.[27]

Dan West believed that his work during the Spanish Civil War was the moral equivalent to military service. The peace churches should create a "relief machine," he said, which would be "under civilian not military control." It would engage "in a non-partisan relief in wartime. . . . We can earn the right to ask for exemption from military duty if we get busy on jobs such as these. . . . Our record . . . will be a better argument than our intentions, however sincere, without that record."[28]

The Continuation Committee of the historic peace churches kept up a steady flow of activity during the years from 1936 to 1939. While the actual consequence of much of the work was probably ephemeral, the matter of importance was that when war came in 1939, the key actors had been in active association with each other for several years. They understood each other and the spirit of warm fellowship and trust that had developed in the half-decade prior to 1940 set a tone for the cooperative work of wartime.

Each of the peace churches continued an ongoing dialogue about the form of service which could be hoped for if war came. By the late 1930s the common consensus, as Mennonite Guy Hershberger put it, was that "if in a future war there is any provision for exemption from military service it will probably be due to the fact that the nonresistant people themselves devised the plan."[29] Both the Mennonites and the Brethren worked at the development of possible plans.

Early in 1935 the Mennonite Peace Problems Committee sponsored a conference for (Old) Mennonites at Goshen College. In the midst of nonstop speeches by nearly every "weighty" Mennonite in the church, a paper by Goshen College professor Guy Hershberger stands out as particularly insightful regarding the imminent future. The paper was entitled "Is Alternative Service Desirable and Possible?"

After examining several other options—military service, noncombatancy, and absolute refusal of all service—Hershberber found a number of desirable advantages in alternative service.

War is a time of suffering, he said. It behooves Christians to render service to those who suffer. Alternative service offers a Christian witness. It offers a graphic alternative way of behaving to that of the world at war. Finally, nationalism and militarism are sweeping the world. The United States government may in the next war, as in the last one, find it very difficult to acknowledge the claims of nonresistance. By having a plan of alternative service the church can make credible claim for consideration even in the midst of the hysteria of war.

Hershberger pointed to both the Russian Mennonite Forestry Service and the Friends reconstruction units as models. He believed the American Civilian Conservation Corps might serve as a context for a program such as he had outlined. He urged that Mennonites move immediately to plan and prepare a program for the government to consider.[30]

In 1935 the Brethren annual conference created the Committee on Legal Counsel for Conscientious Objectors. The committee brought a detailed report to annual conference in 1938. Brethren conscientious objectors could perform service of a constructive nature under either church or civilian direction. The report listed types of service "not consistent with the historic position of the church": military chaplaincy, YMCA under the military, military hospital work, Red Cross work under military auspices, and military service.

In an unusual move, the report also called all Brethren to refrain from war bond purchases, to renounce wartime profits, and to refuse to pay war taxes. A plan of action called for the presentation of the Brethren program to all levels of government and a commitment from the church to assist all members who suffered for the sake of conscience.[31]

The plan of action was written by Rufus D. Bowman, Paul H. Bowman, F. S. Carpes, C. Ray Keim, M. R. Zigler, Dan West, and Ross D. Murphy—all active in peace work with World War I Brethren conscientious objectors. The report was an admirable remedy for the defects encountered during the war, but Rufus Bowman, chairman of the committee, admitted that it probably ran well ahead of general Church of the Brethren conviction. The committee had "talked through the problem, but had not educated the church to any extent," he remarked.

Nevertheless, the annual conference endorsed the plan, but as the statement circulated to the churches it was soon evident that much teaching and education was still necessary to make the statement truly the opinion of the church laity.[32]

Meanwhile, the meetings of the historic peace church representatives and the sharing of ideas and plans continued. In a historic peace church conference in Chicago in March 1938, the Brethren presented "Our Group Procedure in a War Crisis." The statement requested the historic peace churches "to plan together, to work together, and if necessary, to suffer together." Registration for the draft and alternative service options were also discussed. Dan West proposed the creation of a historic peace church Youth Council, a good idea never acted upon.[33]

The historic peace church work in the interwar period was largely inconclusive. Perhaps its most formative benefit was that it brought together a group of people who thought and worked at peace and war issues and schooled them for the demanding times immediately ahead with the onset of World War II. They learned about each other's idiosyncrasies and the ways their own histories and theologies affected their perceptions of peace and war.

The key matter around which they shared most easily was alternative service. In truth, without that central concern the "historic peace church" designation would have little portent. As it was, it was the issue which kept them coming together, and when the European war began in the fall of 1939, the historic peace churches had the organizations, lines of communication, and people in key places to take on the arduous tasks ahead.

They also had a general consensus regarding the shape and form of a desirable alternative service. It should be under civilian direction, of significant moral value, and of sufficient challenge to counter the wartime coaxing of patriotism and war hysteria. Alternative service should be, as Clarence Pickett saw it, the "moral equivalent of war."[34]

Alternative Service and the Absolutists

The German invasion of Poland in August 1939 served as a catalyst prompting action by the leaders of the historic peace churches. The war they had anticipated was now at hand and the conversations between the historic peace churches in previous years, while fruitful and amicable, now faced the test of wartime conditions. With the declaration of war by Britain, Canadian Mennonites were suddenly confronted with the issue of conscription. Harold S. Bender, on behalf of the Mennonite Peace Problems Committee, spent the first week of September 1939 in Ontario, advising Mennonite church leaders on conscientious objection issues.[35]

In a letter to M. R. Zigler on September 14, Harold Bender indicated Mennonite intentions: "Mennonites . . . are definitely planning to carry out a program of alternative service, and are interested in what other groups are doing along this line."[36]

The continuation committee of the historic peace churches committee met on September 17 in Goshen, Indiana, to explore next steps. The committee addressed three issues: a possible interview with President Roosevelt, the question of a common relief effort in Europe, and the desirability of developing a united historic peace church position on conscription.

The sense of the meeting was to plan for an interview with President Roosevelt as soon as possible. The committee decided to create a joint delegation carrying a common statement to the president. Each group would develop a document to be submitted to the others. A meeting to consolidate the material was to follow.[37]

The Mennonites met in Chicago on September 30 under the auspices of the newly created Mennonite Central Peace Committee, a steering committee representing each of the major Mennonite groups. The "Plan of Action" developed at this meeting became the basic document later presented to the president. The plan urged registration, but enjoined young men to indicate their conscientious objection to military service at the point of registration. It also proposed alternative service for conscientious objectors under civilian control, "acceptable to our Christian conscience and conformable to the principles of the Gospel."[38]

During October the historic peace churches continuation committee met frequently to hammer out a common document. Harold Bender reported to Professor E. L. Harshbarger of Bethel College on October 26 that he, Rufus Bowman of the Church of the Brethren, and Rufus Jones and Robert Balderston of the Friends met earlier in the week in Chicago and agreed "substantially" on the Mennonite plan of action. "Rufus Jones stands foursquare for the program which we have outlined," Bender reported. (Jones was making the arrangements for the meeting with the president.)[39]

On November 1 Robert Balderston reported to Ray Wilson of the American Friends Service Committee that besides alternative work, the statement would commit the historic peace churches to relief and service work in peacetime. Balderston hoped the precedent of the Friends work in World War I would serve as a convincing model.[40]

Just as the work appeared to be nearing completion, a complication emerged which was to continue as a matter of contention for the duration of the historic peace church collaboration on conscription. By early December the draft document had circulated to most of the constituent groups for their approval. The arduous search for a common statement on conscription appeared to have been achieved.

But it was not to be. Robert Balderston, the Chicago-based Friends representative, was in almost continuous contact with Harold Bender and Rufus Bowman. But his liaison with the American Friends Service Committee in Philadelphia was often tenuous. It came as a considerable surprise, therefore, to learn that the American Friends Service Committee had strong reservations about a statement to the president which did not support those conscientious objectors who would adopt an absolutist position on the draft, including refusal to register.

In a December 7 letter to the ad hoc committee preparing for the visit to the president, American Friends Service Committee staffer Raymond Wilson argued that the proposed statement should speak on behalf of the absolutists as well as those who could accept alternative service. He reported that he and his colleague at the American Friends Service Committee, Ray Newton, had reflected their concerns to both Harold Bender and Rufus Jones, and the latter approved "heartily."

"If the three historic peace churches can ask for broad enough policies, then each will be free to promote its own particular emphasis within that scope," he argued.[41]

Harold Bender disagreed and summarized the Mennonite position in his usual direct fashion. He could not, in good conscience, return to the constituent Mennonite groups and gain their assent to an issue as divisive as absolute conscientious objection. To do so would result in a long colloquy which would almost certainly end inconclusively. Furthermore, the statement as it stood emphasized the positive expression of service. He questioned, as he put it, "the negative position of the absolutist which runs diametrically counter to the philosophy which we have been operating on so far."

Bender believed the statement should be as simple and the issues as few as possible. The absolutist position would immensely complicate the presentation. He went on to argue:

> This is not to say, however, that the delegation has no concern for the absolutist, or is not willing to do its best to protect their interests and consciences. I personally would be willing to go a long way to help those who in all Christian conscience feel they must take this position. However I feel this must be incidental to our presentation to the president and not a major part of it. Frankly I see nothing for the absolutist, except to accept the consequences and take imprisonment, and therefore feel that there is little that can be done.[42]

Bender's argument is a good example of one side of the issue which would emerge again during the summer of 1940 as the historic peace churches lobbied for a clause recognizing conscientious objectors in the Burke-Wadsworth Selective Service bill.

After a meeting of Balderston, Bender, and Bowman, Balderston reported to Wilson that the three agreed that "it would be a mistake" to revise the document. The stress must remain on alternative service as a "positive expression of Christian goodwill." They proposed, Balderston reported, to take up the issue of the absolutist with Attorney General Murphy after the visit to the president.[43]

But Wilson and his American Friends Service Committee colleagues were not to be put off easily. "I wonder," Wilson remarked to Balderston, "if to some of our young people the proposed statement will not smack very much of the historic peace churches trying to be quite sure to save their skins from the rigors of conscription without too much thought of either what influence it might have on public opinion or the war itself." Noting the Mennonite position, he continued: "I suppose there is something of irony in the fact that the Mennonites who have looked askance at our emphasis on political action and political participation, now find us wondering why they are unwilling to go to a logical extreme of political noncooperation in time of war."[44]

It was the unanimous opinion of the Peace Section of the American Friends Service Committee, Wilson reported, that unless the absolutist position was included, the Friends should not be included in the planned visit to the president. Meanwhile, Rufus Jones was also changing his mind. On December 29 he visited Wilson to reflect his concern over the impasse.[45]

Robert Balderston was the man caught in the middle of the controversy. Writing on New Year's Day, 1940, he reminded Wilson of how much work had gone into preparation of the document the Peace Section was now prepared to scuttle. "I feel sure the Peace Section does not realize how close we have come, through this last-minute suggestion, to wrecking all our five years' work in building closer and closer collaboration and understanding." He also observed that Rufus Bowman of the Church of the Brethren reported strong agreement by his constituents with the Mennonite position.[46]

Time was running out. The White House announced the interview of the historic peace church delegation with the president for January 10. The impasse had to be resolved quickly. Finally all parties agreed to take two documents to the president. One was a general statement highlighting the peace stance of the historic peace churches and urging initiatives which would avoid the lamentable confusion and suffering experienced during World War I. The second statement was a confidential memorandum outlining specific procedures to be used with conscientious objectors, including a paragraph on the absolutist position and another on behalf of conscientious objectors who were not members of the historic peace churches. The statements were signed by Rufus Jones, Walter C. Woodward, E. L. Harshbarger, Harold S. Bender, P. C. Hiebert, Rufus D. Bowman, and Paul Bowman.[47]

The visit to President Roosevelt went well. Affable and charming, he quickly put the delegation at ease, and like so many delegations before them, sent them away feeling that their visit had been a significant success. Of symbolic value, it had little substantive importance. Until very late in 1940, and then only cryptically and capriciously, the president would play no active role whatsoever in historic peace church concerns. The churchmen overestimated the significance of the visit. P. C. Hiebert, representing the Mennonite Brethren, commented to E. L. Harshbarger, "I visualize an almost incalculable amount of suffering and heartache warded off. May it be so!"[48]

The real benefit was the new awareness by the Mennonites and Brethren of the deep concern of many Friends for the absolutist position. All parties subscribed to the service motif for alternative service. But on the issue of absolutism, there was at best an uneasy truce. The episode highlights a fundamental assumption of the Mennonites and Brethren and some Friends: that historic peace church conscientious objectors owed some form of nonmilitary service to the nation under a conscription law.

CHAPTER 4

The Struggle for Alternative Service in 1940

"We are also happy in the change made in the conscientious objector clause in the conscription bill, and as usual must give the Quakers credit for having carried through the brunt of this. As a church we appreciate this help from the Friends very much."
—Orie Miller, August 1940

New Organizations

Spring 1940 found the historic peace churches concentrating on new organizations, educational programs, and a variety of representations to government bodies regarding draft issues. The Mennonites created a new coordinating group—the Mennonite Central Peace Committee—in September 1939. The Mennonite Central Peace Committee had representatives from most of the major Mennonite groups. Its role was to coordinate Mennonite peace concerns. The Mennonite Central Peace Committee eventually evolved into the Peace Section of the Mennonite Central Committee. During 1940 this committee played a major role in inter-Mennonite peace efforts.

The Brethren took the first steps in creating what came to be known as the Brethren Service Committee in November 1939. The five-member committee was to coordinate relief and peace efforts for the Church of the Brethren.

The Friends established the War Problems Committee in 1940 to monitor and influence draft legislation before and during the legislative process, inform Friends of issues and developments regarding conscription, and advise young Friends in regard to conscription. The eight-member Committee became a counterpart of the Mennonite Central Peace Committee and the Brethren Service Committee. During the long summer of 1940 and in the early months of the Civilian Public Service program, the War Problems Committee was a key group shaping the course of the emerging alternative service program.

The Mennonite Central Peace Committee appointed Orie O. Miller to serve as its representative in conscientious objector matters in Washington. In June 1940 he began an active liaison role in conjunction with Friends and Brethren activity in the nation's capital. At the invitation of M. R. Zigler, newly appointed executive secretary of the Brethren Service Committee, Miller attended Brethren Service Committee meetings dealing with conscription. In May, Harold S. Bender of the Mennonite Central Peace Committee attended the first meeting of the newly established Federal Council of Churches' Coordinating Committee on the Conscientious Objector.

The untimely death of Robert Balderston in April 1940 deprived the historic peace churches of a key member of the continuation committee. As we have seen, Balderston played a role as mediator and bridge between the three churches. Less venturesome and aggressive than his American Friends Service Committee colleagues, he shared the basic convictions of the Mennonites and Brethren. Errol Elliott, pastor of the First Friends Church of Indianapolis, replaced Balderston on the continuation committee.

Historic Peace Churches in Washington

The historic peace churches continued their efforts to keep their concerns before the administration in Washington, but their efforts tended to be episodic and uncoordinated. On June 6, Dan West, Orie Miller, and Clarence Pickett met with Solicitor General Francis Biddle to further clarify understandings regarding historic peace church conscription concerns. As we will discover, the solicitor general had no connection at all with the emerging draft legislation.

The historic peace churches were keenly concerned to keep the conscientious objector issue under civilian control. Relying on administration assurances to that effect, they were putting their efforts into largely fruitless initiatives. Had Biddle sought to misdirect historic peace church energies he could not have done so more successfully. Perhaps he did so by design.

In any case, during the interview on June 6, he requested that each of the historic peace churches conduct a census of draft-age men and report the results to him. The Friends and Brethren responded coolly to the idea. The Mennonites took the request seriously and on June 17, during a meeting of the Mennonite Central Peace Committee at North Newton, Kansas, arrangements were made for each Mennonite group to conduct a careful census.[1]

This episode was characteristic of historic peace church-government relationships prior to the emergence of the Burke-Wadsworth Selective Service Bill. The administration had almost no interest in a conscription bill; in fact, actively opposed such a bill. The historic peace churches believed conscription would eventually occur. Burdened by their memories of World War I, they felt a strong urgency to avoid being "caught unprepared as last time."[2] As a result, historic peace church urgency in the spring of 1940 was usually met by a lethargic, and in Biddle's case, diversionary response.

Historic Peace Church Conferences

Both the Brethren and the Friends held their annual conferences in June. Clarence Pickett of the American Friends Service Committee was the keynote speaker at the Brethren Conference at Ocean Grove, New Jersey. In his address he highlighted historic peace church cooperation on peace issues. The Brethren Conference assigned M. R. Zigler, Paul H. Bowman, and Ross D. Murphy as a special "Advisory Committee for Conscientious Objectors" to represent the Brethren interests in Washington. The Conference also assigned the Brethren Service Committee to continue its role of interpreting peace issues to the congregations.[3]

The Friends General Conference met at Cape May, New Jersey, in early July. Prior to that meeting, an important Friends meeting occurred on the campus of

Earlham College in Richmond, Indiana. From July 2-4 twenty-two Yearly Meetings of Friends from across the nation met to discuss the Quaker response to conscription. Most of the leaders of the American Friends Service Committee and many Philadelphia Friends were in attendance. The chair of the conference, Randolph Pyle, observed that in World War I Friends were not prepared for the emergency. He hoped that a more thoughtful and measured response could be made to what appeared to be a newly emerging war.

A highlight of the conference was the report by Clarence Pickett on recent developments. Pickett had just met with Attorney General Murphy and Sidney Hillman. Hillman was to be the liaison with groups concerned with draft issues. Neither Murphy nor Hillman believed the new Burke-Wadsworth Selective Service Bill would pass. Nor did they believe any action on conscription would occur before the November presidential election. Hillman personally opposed a compulsory draft. Pickett reported that President Roosevelt had assured him that "we are trying to keep this thing [draft] on a voluntary basis."

Pickett noted that he had conveyed to all his government contacts in Washington the Friends conviction that young people ought to contribute time and energy—without compensation—to the public welfare. The precedent he pointed to was the Friends work camp program which offered young people an opportunity for service. Above all, Pickett insisted to his conferees, Friends must move beyond concern for "Quaker skins" to concern for "Quaker consciences." Quakers must get out of the "niche we are in, of nice people with a conscience, letting the Navy protect us."

Pickett's comments set the stage for two intensive days of Quaker dialogue, beautifully preserved in minutes which capture the cadence and rhythm of the meeting, as the eighty persons in attendance searched for consensus on the major issues of compulsory conscription. The findings committee report summarized the result: opposition to all forms of conscription; concern that all Friends engage in meaningful peace and humanitarian work, regardless of the international situation; the special responsibility of Friends to help reduce war hysteria and defend civil rights in their local communities; and the need to discover opportunities for special assistance to war sufferers in the conflicts then raging in Europe and Asia.[4]

Thus by July 1940 each of the historic peace churches had designed new organizational groups to represent their conscription concerns. They had gained valuable experience from a variety of encounters with government officials and agencies in Washington. And they pursued useful interchurch conversations regarding conscription issues.

From the vantage point of hindsight, the historic peace churches were uniquely ready for the challenging and arduous events which were to unfold during the summer and autumn of 1940. A providential convergence of leadership, organization, and events had transpired. The two-decade effort to avert a replay of the traumatic World War I experience of the historic peace churches had succeeded.

However before the story of the passage of the Burke-Wadsworth Bill and the design of the Civilian Public Service program is told, one last series of events must be relayed to set the stage.

Military Preparedness

France fell before the onslaught of Adolf Hitler's blitz-krieg in June 1940, after an astounding series of quick and successful German assaults on the Scandinavian and Low Countries in April and May. England, preserved behind the English Channel, awaited Hitler's next move. Few doubted that England was his next quarry.

President Roosevelt's sympathies ran strongly to the British, but he was uncertain about the American political climate. Nineteen forty was a presidential election year. The political conventions loomed on the horizon. The troublesome course of events abroad, coupled with the prevailing mood of neutrality (or isolationism) in the United States created a politically unstable situation which he responded to by biding his time.

He knew only too well the unprepared condition of the American military machine. The army, in May 1940, consisted of 200,000 men armed with World War I weapons. The air corps was even more flaccid. The navy, second largest in the world, rode on WWI-vintage ships.

Roosevelt made several tentative moves in the direction of preparedness. On May 16 he requested $1.2 billion in military appropriations to build a new fleet of war planes. Two weeks later he asked for an additional supplement of $1.3 billion for a new army and a two-ocean navy. Congress, still isolationist, nevertheless voted the money with only minimal resistance. But the isolationism of the country ran deep, and the president's limited action was strongly conditioned by the fact that three out of the four Republican contenders for the nomination for president—Dewey, Taft, and Vandenberg—were isolationists.

Of all the defense issues, military manpower was the

most volatile. The specter of a new American expeditionary force was political dynamite. At the news conference announcing the naval rearmament program on May 28, the president put all of his stress on arms and equipment. "We are not talking at the present time about a draft system, either to draft men, women, or money, or all three."[5]

Chief of Staff George Marshall did not believe a compulsory military draft in peacetime could be enacted in Congress. Nor was he convinced of the necessity of a draft in peacetime. In fact he did not want a draft because the army was unprepared logistically to handle the large number of recruits such a system would generate.

During the interwar period, the American military establishment was exceedingly cautious. Very little effort was expended in long-range manpower planning. In 1922 the personnel division of the general staff of the army, under the direction of Lt. Col. M. C. Krimer, proposed a skeletal Selective Service System. The Chief of Staff created a Joint Army and Navy Selective Service Committee in 1926 to take responsibility for conscription legislation if it were to be needed. The committee operated on the presumption that the World War I Selective Service law was basically successful and should serve as a model for the future.

In 1937, as international order deteriorated, the army adopted the "Protective Mobilization Plan" whereby the volunteer regular army would serve as a protective force until mobilization of a large conscripted army could be effected. The army believed it would have ample time to enact the conscription plan after hostilities began.[6]

Military planners were also impressed by the powerful civilian pacifist currents of the 1930s. They simply did not believe conscription legislation could be passed by

Congress in peacetime. The Joint Army and Navy Committee, chaired in 1940 by Major Lewis B. Hershey, assumed that draft legislation would not be presented to Congress until Congress had actually declared war. As a stop-gap measure, the Joint Committee had a plan—the Civilian Volunteer Effort—whereby each state governor would direct an aggressive volunteer recruitment effort until Congress could enact the Joint Committee's compulsory conscription plan.[7]

Thus, in late spring of 1940, neither the Joint Committee nor the president contemplated the imminent enactment of a military conscription law. Yet within five months a new law was passed and an elaborate new structure was created to mobilize American manpower for a war which was at that point still more than a year in the future.

What precipitated the changed prospects for the military draft is one of the obscure, but fascinating, stories which emerge from time to time in American history.

The Military Training Camps Association Offensive

As the German army began its advance into the Low Countries in early May 1940, a small group of men met at the Harvard Club in New York City to plan the twenty-fifth anniversary of the Military Training Camps Association. The Military Training Camps Association was an organization created in 1915 as part of the Plattsburg Movement to get the United States involved in preparation for entry into the European war.

A primary concern was the training of officers. The Plattsburg group was alarmed at the dearth of officers in the regular army in 1915 and fearful of the consequences should the United States be forced into a combat situation. The Military Training Camps Association solution was a crash program to train an officer corps to fill the perceived gap.

A raucous and somewhat undisciplined movement in World War I, the group was led by wealthy Easterners whose foresight in 1915 was sufficiently vindicated by events in 1916 and following, that they had not only gained respectability, but a strong sense of camaraderie. Hence, the annual reunions, and now, in 1940 the planning for a twenty-fifth anniversary celebration.[8]

Participants at the May 8 meeting in the elegant quarters of the Harvard Club in New York City were Phillip Carroll, New York City lawyer; Julius Ochs Adler, general manager of the *New York Times;* Langdon D. Marvin, former law partner of Franklin Delano Roosevelt; T. Lloyd Derby, son-in-law of Theodore Roosevelt; Grenville Clark, member of the law firm of Root, Clark, et al; A. L. Boyce, president of the Military Training Camps Association; and Alfred Rollker, secretary of the Military Training Camps Association.

Grenville Clark was an ardent advocate of American intervention in the broadening European conflict. He was becoming increasingly concerned by the emerging Nazi campaign in the Low Countries. His vivid memories of the 1914 invasion of Belgium by Germany were now given almost spectral form as the Germans advanced into the Netherlands and Belgium.

In the course of the meeting, Clark rose and commented on the new emergency. He proposed that the Military Training Camps Association be true to its history and become the advocate for a new compulsory training and service program.

Clark's speech found immediate support. The group drew up three resolutions: to advocate compulsory military training and service, to urge immediate United States aid to the European allies, and to lobby for a program to train pilots. Clark was made the chair of a committee to plan the next meeting. His committee was enjoined to invite persons of stature to the meeting scheduled for May 22 to plan the next steps in implementing the resolutions.[9]

Clark did not disappoint his colleagues. Attending the May 22 meeting were nearly 100 of the leading Eastern Seaboard interventionists, including Henry L. Stimson, former secretary of state; Elihu Root, former secretary of state and secretary of war; Robert P. Patterson, future secretary of war; Frank Knox, soon to be secretary of the navy; and General Ryan of the National Guard, among others. Out of the meeting came a new group, the National Emergency Committee of the Military Training Camps Association. Its mandate was to promote as rapidly as possible the creation and enactment by Congress of a compulsory conscription program.[10]

Clark was elected chair of the New Emergency Committee. The next morning (May 23) he sent General M. A. Palmer of the Military Training Camps Association to Washington to press for army support. Palmer visited Chief of Staff George C. Marshall and Major Lewis B. Hershey of the Joint Army and Navy Committee.

To his surprise, he found strong opposition to the military training camps proposals. Several days of discussion ensued. Major Hershey and Captain Weible of the Joint Army and Navy Committee even traveled to New York City to hear the Military Training Camps Association arguments. But the army was not impressed with the urgency of the situation. In desperation, Grenville Clark and Julius Ochs Adler flew to Washington on May 31 to confront General Marshall directly and enlist the army in the Military Training Camps Association program.[11]

Marshall stubbornly resisted the arguments of Clark and Adler. He insisted that Congress would not countenance a peacetime draft and that the Joint Army and Navy Committee civilian volunteer effort would serve adequately until legislation could be passed after a declaration of war. More importantly, Marshall was seeking an enormous increase in the military appropriations budget and could not afford to jeopardize the pending legislation. Finally, in an oblique reference to the political problems of his commander in chief, Marshall observed that it was the president, not the chief of staff, who should take action on military manpower legislation.[12]

Failing to convince Marshall, Clark and Adler then sought a meeting with the president. In this they also failed.

Finally, convinced that the key problem was weak leadership at the war department, Clark visited Supreme Court Justice Frankfurter. He persuaded Frankfurter, a close confidant of Roosevelt, that what was needed was the appointment of Henry L. Stimson as secretary of war. Frankfurter approached the president, pointing out the political benefits Roosevelt could garner by appointing a ranking leader of the Republican Party to a high cabinet post in a political year.

Frankfurter had little difficulty convincing the president. Stimson would be the next secretary of war. Beyond even Clark's hopes, Roosevelt also agreed to appoint Republican Frank Knox—editor of the *Chicago Daily*

News, former Roughrider, and devotee of military pre-paredness—as Secretary of the Navy.[13]

On June 3, the day Roosevelt agreed to Stimson as secretary of war, the New Emergency Committee met in Julius Ochs Adler's office at the *New York Times*. Clark and Adler reported on their successful trip to Washington, D.C. Later in the day they met with 200 Military Training Camps Association members to present their plan of action.

Theirs was an ambitious plan: to write a manpower conscription bill, find sponsors for it in Congress, and build public support via newspapers and radio. Already Parley Boone, a highly regarded public relations expert, had been retained for the public relations efforts. A budget of $285,000 was agreed upon, to be raised from private sources.[14]

The text of the proposed legislation was completed within the week. On June 11, Howard Peterson, Clark's aide, delivered copies of the Military Training Camps Association plan to the White House, to Generals Marshall and Pershing, and to the Joint Army and Navy Selective Service Committee.[15]

The next step was to find congressional sponsorship for the legislation. The Military Training Camps Association choice of sponsor in the House was a natural: Representative James E. Wolcott Wadsworth of New York.

Wadsworth had a long history as an advocate of military conscription and the citizen army. As he observed to Wendell Willkie, "I confess to have been a crank on this subject for many years."[16]

In 1920, as a senator and chair of the Senate Committee on Military Affairs, he had worked industriously to create a national defense force based on conscription. Wadsworth had collaborated with the Military Training Camps Association during the 1920s to create a volunteer program called the Citizen's Military Training Camps Movement which trained civilians in military arts. The Military Training Camps Association served as the recruiter for the Citizen's Military Training Force. By 1936 half a million men had participated in the program.[17] The connections between the Military Training Camps Association and Wadsworth were thus natural and obvious.

Finding a Senate sponsor proved more difficult because of the political problems inherent in the draft program, but eventually Senator Edward R. Burke of Nebraska agreed to cosponsor the legislation, which quickly became known as the Burke-Wadsworth Bill. The president disliked the choice of sponsors because Burke had a long record of opposition to the New Deal and Wadsworth was a Republican.[18]

The Burke-Wadsworth Bill

On June 20 as the Germans entered Paris, the Burke-Wadsworth Selective Service Bill was introduced in the Senate. That afternoon Henry Stimson became the new secretary of war. Frank Knox joined Stimson in the cabinet as secretary of the navy. The day before, Stimson had told a Yale University audience that he favored universal military training and massive American assistance to the Allies.[19]

Burke-Wadsworth was now in the legislative arena. It had not yet been accepted by the armed forces. General Marshall, in light of the German successes in Europe, intended to put the Civilian Volunteer Effort into effect, for he did not believe Burke-Wadsworth could pass the Congress. Marshall's action would surely have destroyed Burke-Wadsworth. Stimson, in one of his first acts as secretary of war, overrode Marshall and abolished the Civilian Volunteer Effort.[20]

The Joint Army and Navy Selective Service Committee was not enthusiastic about the Burke-Wadsworth Bill. They considered it too complicated. Their reservations were so serious that they prepared to sharply criticize the bill in their testimony before the Senate and House committees.

To avert that possibility, Grenville Clark arranged a conference with Stimson which included members of the Joint Committee, several Military Training Camps Association representatives, and members of the National Guard Association. Out of that session emerged a revision satisfactory to all parties.

On June 30 Stimson wrote Senator Sheppard, chair of the Senate Committee on Military Affairs, urging passage of the newly revised bill. The army had finally come to the support of the Burke-Wadsworth Selective Service Bill.[21]

Thus the stage was set for the next phase of the historic peace church struggle to secure freedom of conscience for conscientious objectors to military conscription. The new bill made reference to conscientious objection to military service using language almost identical to that used in the 1917 conscription legislation:

> Section 7 (d). Nothing contained in this Act shall be construed to require or compel any person to be subject to training or service in a combatant capacity in the land or

naval forces who is found to be a member of any well recognized sect whose creed or principles forbid its members to participate in war in any form, if the conscientious holding of such belief by such person shall be established under such regulations as the President may prescribe; but no such person shall be relieved from training or service in such capacity as the President may declare to be noncombatant.[22]

Section 7 (d) provided an ominous reminder to the historic peace church leaders that unless they acted with resolution, the experience of the conscientious objector in World War I might well be repeated. It also suggested that the efforts thus far expended had not had much effect. New strategies were needed.

The Historic Peace Church Legislative Offensive

The text of the Burke-Wadsworth Selective Service Bill was published in many newspapers, including the *New York Times,* thanks to the efforts of Parley Boone, publicity agent for the Military Training Camps Association. Senator Sheppard, chair of the Senate Committee on Military Affairs, announced that hearings on the pending legislation would begin on July 3.

The historic peace churches had the text of the bill available, but very little time to consult together regarding the issues at hand. The result was a lack of coordinated effort in the early stages. For example, it was not until July 12 that Orie Miller, on behalf of the Mennonite Central Peace Committee, contacted Senator Sheppard for an opportunity to testify regarding Mennonite conscientious objector concerns. Sheppard replied that he would have been glad to hear from the Mennonites, but the hearings had been concluded.[23]

The Friends were more resourceful. The Central Committee of the Friends General Conference met at Cape May, New Jersey, on July 8, 1940. There the Social Order Committee reviewed the pending Burke-Wadsworth Bill. The Committee formulated a strong statement opposing the bill and dispatched Paul C. French on the afternoon of July 9 to Washington to testify on their behalf before the Senate committee the next day.

The statement, signed by Arthur C. Jackson, chair of the Central Committee, Friends General Conference, denounced all military conscription as a fundamental violation of constitutional rights. This initial response—to work for the defeat of the Bill—suggests that as of July 10 the historic peace churches were not totally clear who their opponents were.

In the following weeks the powerful coalition favoring the draft would become clearly evident and the historic peace church campaign would become much more pragmatic. Instead of attempting to defeat the whole bill, the historic peace churches would try to tailor the conscientious objector provisions to encompass their special concerns.

The statement of the Cape May Friends General Conference was less important in retrospect than the fact that this event signaled the emergence during the next six months of Paul C. French as the primary coordinator and lobbyist to modify the conscientious objector provisions in the Burke-Wadsworth Bill.

French was remarkably well-prepared for the assignment. A birthright Friend, he worked for many years as a reporter. Just prior to 1940 he had served for three years as director of the Federal Writer Project. He was thus already oriented to the ways of Washington, D.C., and had acquired a knack for ferreting out information and making timely contacts. Above all he understood who the real decision-makers were and how to best influence their actions.

Furthermore, during 1939 he wrote a timely book entitled *We Won't Murder* which reviewed the experience of conscientious objectors in World War I and critiqued the American government's handling of conscientious objectors. He concluded that the "best method of handling conscientious objectors to war becomes one of unconditional and unqualified exemption from all conscription for either military or so-called alternative civilian service."[24] The book received considerable attention in Friends circles and as the conscription emergency developed French rapidly moved to the fore as a spokesperson for the Friends.

Working with French during the summer of 1940 was Raymond Wilson, associate secretary of the American Friends Service Committee Peace Section. Wilson was a strong proponent of the absolute exemption position. Wilson emerged during the conscription legislation arguments as the most articulate spokesperson for historic peace church concerns. His testimony before the Senate and House committees was crisp and forthright. French, who knew the corridors of power, and Wilson, who spoke the historic peace church vision, were an excellent team.

As the board of directors of the American Friends Service Committee became more aware of the conscription bill in June, Edward Evans and others urged the creation of a special committee to deal with the specific conscription issue. A ten-person committee was established by the

American Friends Service Committee board during the last week of June and became known as the Friends War Problems Committee. In early July the committee hired Paul C. French for three months to carry out its directives in Washington, D.C. In the early weeks of the conscription battle, French worked out of a hotel room, but as it became apparent that the assignment would become more permanent, he proceeded to establish an office.

The original intent of the Friends, as represented in the July 10 statement noted earlier, was to attempt the defeat of the Burke-Wadsworth Bill. That aim, while not abandoned, was soon superseded by a campaign to secure appropriate language to protect the convictions of conscientious objectors.

Section 7 (d) of the original June 20 version of the bill recognized the conscientious objection of only those who were members of a "well recognized religious sect whose creed of principles forbid its members to participate in war in any form." Even those persons meeting that criteria were not exempt from service; it was left to the president to prescribe the appropriate form of noncombatant service. No protection was afforded either general religious or nonreligious conscientious objectors. It was clear that unless the historic peace churches acted decisively, the melancholy experience of World War I would be repeated. Certainly no one in government would intervene to change the language and the larger religious bodies lacked credibility on the issue even had any chosen to act.

The historic peace churches took the initiative. At the request of the Friends War Problems Committee, Harold Evans wrote an amendment incorporating five elements the peace churches considered essential to their interests:

1. A register of conscientious objectors
2. A civilian Bureau for Conscientious Objectors reporting to the Attorney General
3. Provision for conscientious objectors to do work for national importance under civilian control
4. A national board of appeal
5. A complete exemption for conscientious objectors who refused all service.

A caucus by historic peace church representatives in Paul French's hotel room reviewed the proposal and came to quick agreement. The next day French and Wilson carried the text of the amendment to the Senate Military Affairs Committee. The committee gave the document short shrift—only two members voted in favor of the amendment.[25]

Finding the Senate committee unresponsive to their efforts, French and Wilson then gained permission from General Shedd, deputy chief of staff, to consult with Colonel Victor J. O'Kelliher, the officer at the war department assigned to oversee conscription legislation. They informed O'Kelliher that section 7 (d) as it stood was unacceptable to the historic peace churches, and presented the version just defeated in the Senate committee.

O'Kelliher refused to consider complete exemption for nonregistrants. On the other issues, compromise wordings were worked out. The new version was then discussed by an ad hoc group of Military Affairs Committee senators and General Shedd.

During this session the phrase *religious training and belief* was inserted. The War Problems Committee had avoided reference to a religious basis for conscientious objection in an effort to broaden the bill's scope. Much to the chagrin of French and Wilson, the senators insisted on the inclusion of the religious phrase. The rest of the conditions of the revised version were accepted by the group.[26]

The next day, July 25, French and Wilson presented the compromise version to the House Military Affairs Committee and reported its acceptance by the Senate committee and General Shedd. They made a strong appeal for the inclusion of a clause protecting the absolutist. While they failed to convince the committee on the later point, July 25 was clearly French and Wilson's best day, for they were able to convince the committee to incorporate the essential language of their proposal as presented.[27]

The House Military Affairs Committee held hearings on the bill for eleven days in late July and early August, during some of Washington's hottest weather in many years. Forty-three witnesses testified on behalf of the conscientious objector clause. It was an eloquent testimony to the importance attached to freedom of conscience by American religious and peace organizations.

The work of the historic peace churches was not at an end, however. In August the bill was debated in the House and Senate, and slowly section 7 (d), so laboriously crafted in July, began to change its shape and form.

On August 6 Attorney General Jackson informed Senator Sheppard, chair of the Senate Committee on Military Affairs, that the Department of Justice was not prepared to handle the conscientious objector as stipulated in the bill. Learning that Sheppard was annoyed by the attorney general's decision, French arranged a meeting with Matthew MacGuire, administrative assistant in the Department of Justice.

As a result MacGuire agreed that the department would not press its concerns further until after passage of the bill. French hoped the Justice Department role could be preserved if the department did not press its case further. After an effort on August 7 to have the absolutist clause reintroduced as an amendment to the House bill, French and Wilson decided not to continue pursuing the absolutist effort, fearing that further pressure might jeopardize the rest of the conscientious objector provisions.[28]

French and Wilson were encouraged when Senator Bone of Washington introduced an amendment providing for trials in federal district courts for those who failed to register to report for duty. This meant that, unlike World War I, where the process was a court-martial, the cases would be handled by civilian courts.[29]

A tremendous setback occurred on September 7. Representative Walter of Pennsylvania moved an amendment in the House which took the registration and hearing procedures out of the Department of Justice where the historic peace churches had placed it and put it back in local draft boards. French was bitterly disappointed and noted sadly, "It is curious how a few minutes can undo the work of a month or more."

To add insult to injury, French and Wilson learned that the change was the result of the direct action of Matthew MacGuire, who only a month earlier had assured French and Wilson that the Justice Department would not press the matter further. When confronted by French, MacGuire argued that the Justice Department expected a large number of cases and did not believe they should assume such a large increment of new work.[30]

The new turn of events was fateful for the conscientious

objector cause. Not only were conscientious objectors now at mercy of local boards often swayed by the heat of patriotic passion; great variation in treatment of the conscientious objectors would surely occur.

French immediately approached several representatives, including Chairperson May of the House Committee on Military Affairs. Representative Dewey Short of Missouri agreed to put the original language back into the bill during the Senate-House conference on the bill. Unfortunately, Short was not successful.[31]

French then turned to General Shedd, who had been helpful in the past. Shedd agreed to arrange a meeting between French, Wilson, and Colonel Frank A. Partridge of the war department.

The three met at French's hotel and outlined the problems as they saw them. Partridge was sympathetic, but did not have much to offer. For the first time it became clear to French and Wilson that the real implication of the new development was to place the entire administration of the conscientious objector issue in the hands of the new Selective Service Administration, an organization designed to conscript men for military service and operated by military personnel.[32]

The emergence of this new direction of things was not unappreciated by the war department personnel in charge of planning for conscription. By mid-August 1940 a skeletal national headquarters had been set up comprising twenty-one officers and twenty-eight civilians. An interoffice memo commented on the stage of the conscription legislation. It noted, in reference to the conscientious objector legislation, that "as now taking shape in the Senate Military Affairs Committee, it appears that the *novel* provisions outlined in our July Bulletin are gradually disappearing."[33] The novel provisions were those incorporated in the O'Kelliher compromise of July 24 which provided for a national registry of conscientious objectors under Justice Department jurisdiction.

The extant sources suggest, however, that in July, French and Wilson managed to develop some directions for the emerging conscientious objector legislation. The one clear failure at that point was the unwillingness of Congress or the war department to countenance any recognition of the absolute objector. One striking and disturbing observation is that not one senator or representative emerged as a champion for the historic peace church cause—this in contrast to the situation in the British House of Commons where a number of the members of parliament took strong and forthright pacifist positions.

The absence of a legislative group prepared to press the historic peace church cause was an obstacle of significant proportions. The intuitive impulse of a majority of legislators was hostile, or at best, mildly neutral to conscientious objector concerns. The ability of the historic peace churches to bring their concerns effectively into play was thus especially problematical, particularly when the legislative process reached the full House or Senate debate stage.

All three historic peace churches contributed to the effort during the summer. The records reveal a constant movement of church leaders to Washington to testify before Senate and House committees, to talk to key legislators and government officials, and to consult with each other on the issues. Throughout the summer the historic peace churches experienced surprising unanimity. The major issues were carefully weighed and discussed. At the same time, French and Wilson were given sufficient freedom to take the initiatives necessary for an aggressive campaign for conscientious objector concerns.

The Friends, because of experience, training, and disposition (they embraced intervention in government processes as an integral part of their witness) clearly took the lead. They must be credited with the major effort. The Brethren and Mennonites were well aware of this. Orie Miller reflected this in a letter to Ray Newton: "We are also happy in the change made in the conscientious objector clause in the conscription bill, and as usual must give the Quakers credit for having carried through the brunt of this. As a church we appreciate this help from the Friends very much."[34]

M. R. Zigler of the Brethren observed, "The Friends are doing a most noble job in organizing the movement to give favorable consideration to the conscientious objector in every way."[35]

CHAPTER 5

Civilian Public Service: Experiment in Alternative Service

"Assignees [in the Civilian Public Service camps] can no more expect choice of location or job than can men in the Service. . . . From the time an assignee reports to camp until he is finally released he is under the control of the Director of Selective Service. He ceases to be a free agent and is accountable for all of his time, in camp and out, 24 hours a day. His movements, actions, and conduct are subject to control and regulation."

—Lieutenant Colonel McLean
of Selective Service, 1940

Conscientious Objector Clause Ratified

Franklin Roosevelt, whose support for the Burke-Wadsworth Bill had been at best highly ambivalent, was nominated in late July as the Democratic candidate for president. With that behind him, he felt free politically to move. On August 3, Roosevelt publicly came out in favor of the Burke-Wadsworth Bill for the first time.

Several weeks later, on August 17, the newly nominated Republican candidate for president—Wendell Willkie— endorsed compulsory military conscription in his acceptance speech. A few days later he called for immediate passage of the Burke-Wadsworth Bill.

Willkie neatly solved the president's political problem. In anticipation of the passage of Burke-Wadsworth, Roosevelt created a National Advisory Committee on Selective Service to work with the Joint Army and Navy Selective Service Committee.[1] The next day, August 28, the Burke-Wadsworth Bill was overwhelmingly passed in the Senate.

On August 31, the president ordered the National Guard into active service, a move calculated to help the House make up its mind regarding the urgency of passing favorably on the bill then being debated. On September 7 the the bill was passed by the House. A Senate-House conference group then met for two days to resolve the differences in the two versions. On September 13 the Conference Committee reported out the final bill and the next day both the House and Senate passed the final bill.

On September 16 the president signed the new Selective Training and Service Act into law.

The historic peace churches had cause for satisfaction with the conscientious objector clause, for it was a vast improvement over the language of World War I and the original June Burke-Wadsworth Bill in four distinct areas: (1) conscientious objector exemption was no longer based on sectarian criteria, but on an individual basis linked to religious training and belief; (2) it recognized a class of conscientious objectors who could do no service under the military—hence the provision for work of national importance under civilian directive; (3) it established an appeal process with Department of Justice hearings for contested cases; and (4) it provided for civilian rather than military trial for violators of the act.

The act also had serious shortcomings. Initial classification of objectors was left in the hands of local draft boards; administration of the process would be in the hands of the Selective Service Administration, a military rather than civilian agency; the appeal process was a complicated three-step system involving the local board, the Department of Justice, and an appeal board; and it lacked any consideration for the absolute objector. Of most immediate concern was the failure to define work of national importance.[2]

Organizing for Action

With the passage of the Selective Training and Service Act, a new phase of peace church cooperation began. On September 4 a group of five Mennonites, six Friends, five Brethren, and Walter Van Kirk of the Federal Council of Churches met at the Commodore Hotel in Washington to survey the work ahead. The key issue addressed was the shape of alternative service. Who will operate the program? Under what jurisdiction? Shall the peace churches cooperate or go their own way? How will it be financed? Should the peace churches take government money?

Several practical initiatives were determined. The group requested Paul French to remain in Washington for another sixty days to give leadership to the new phase. The Mennonites and Brethren would each send a representa-

tive to join French, and the three would constitute a committee representing peace church concerns in the capital.
One of the first assignments given the new committee was
the publication of a manual explaining the new
conscientious objector regulations. Finally the group
agreed to hold a more extended meeting in Chicago on
October 5 to be convened by M. R. Zigler of the Church of
the Brethren.[3]

One of the fascinating elements of the unfolding drama
during the next several months was the degree to which
the peace churches ran ahead of the government in
developing plans for the new conscientious objector
program. Impatient to get to work, French, Orie Miller,
Warren D. Bowman, and Walter Van Kirk arranged a
meeting with General Shedd, deputy chief of staff, to discuss how to begin the work.

It became clear that Shedd did not have much to offer,
and in fact would not be seriously involved in conscientious
objector matters. A few days later they met with Colonel
Frank Partridge from the manpower section of the general
staff and again received friendly advice. But Partridge was
not knowledgeable or responsible for the program.

On September 17, Clarence Pickett, Harold Evans, and
French interviewed Frederick Osborne. Osborne was the
chairperson of a committee newly appointed by President
Roosevelt to review all administrative regulations dealing
with the Selective Service System before they were put into
effect. Osborne promised cooperation, but did not think his
committee would be closely involved in the development
of the program. He did agree that French might want to
stay in contact with Eldridge Sibley, secretary of the
Osborne Committee.[4]

Finally French, Wilson, and Evans met with Colonel Hershey, executive for the Joint Army and Navy Selective Service Committee. Hershey promised that if he became director of Selective Service he would work very hard to give the conscientious objectors every consideration. Hershey gave some constructive if unofficial advice: "Get your groups together and draw up some proposals. No one in the government has given much thought to the problem."[5]

The vague cooperativeness of these encounters with government officials was apparently misunderstood by French, normally a model of realism. Henry Fast, newly appointed Mennonite representative to assist French and to represent the Mennonite Central Peace Committee in Washington, reported on September 19 that French was jubilant. "They practically grant everything asked for. They are eager to make arrangements to safeguard the rights of conscience and to prevent any unnecessary trouble for the conscientious objectors as well as for themselves."[6]

As a result of the series of encounters just outlined, several issues came to the fore. Because the government had not yet had time to address the civilian work program, the historic peace churches had an opportunity to influence the emerging program—*if* they could develop a proposal.

Second, the peace churches needed a common body to represent them during this critical period of planning.

A third issue had to do with funding. Who would finance the program? Before a plan could be designed, the organizational question had to be addressed.

During these weeks the unique character of the three groups became apparent. The Mennonites instinctively

desired their own operation. The Brethren were ambivalent. The Quakers came forward with an offer to run
the whole program. As the discussion ebbed and flowed,
M. R. Zigler of the Brethren emerged as the figure who
helped the peace churches coalesce. At his initiative, representatives of the historic peace churches met at the Mennonite Home Mission on South Union Street in Chicago on
October 4-5.[7]

Civilian Public Service Is Created

Several developments need to be reviewed in order to
set the October 4-5 meeting in context. On October 1,
Colonel Lewis Hershey became acting director of the Selective Service Administration. On October 2, during a
lengthy conference, he inquired of Paul French whether
the American Friends Service Committee would have any
interest in taking over the civilian service program for
conscientious objectors.

"How much financial support would be needed from
the government under such an arrangement?" he asked.[8]

The next day the Friends War Problems Committee
meeting in Philadelphia made Hershey's question the
main point on its agenda. The committee agreed that if the
government seriously desired a private agency to take
responsibility for alternative service, the assignment should
be accepted. Ray Newton, Peace Section secretary, accom-
panied Paul French to Chicago to present this option to the
peace church assembly there the next day.[9]

The Friends were not the only group thinking about a
program under peace church direction. Dan West of the
Church of the Brethren surfaced a well-developed plan for

a "Brethren Volunteer Service." As he put it, this program might be "a unit of a larger cooperative effort."[10]

While the Mennonites had not generated any plans, it was clear they favored peace church control of the alternative program. On October 4, prior to the peace church meeting, the Mennonite Central Peace Committee met and strongly endorsed a church-directed program.[11]

Thus by the time of the Chicago meeting, the prospect of an alternative service program operated by the peace churches had been thoroughly discussed.

M. R. Zigler of the Church of the Brethren presided at the meeting. Sixty-five peace church representatives were in attendance. Paul French reported on recent developments. The conference addressed two issues: the shape and form of a new agency to represent peace church interests in the period of negotiation with the government; and the form of alternative service.

The group quickly agreed to the formation of a new organization, tentatively called the National Council for Religious Conscientious Objectors (later known as the National Service Board for Religious Objectors). On the issue of the alternative service program, consensus was for peace church direction of the program, although it was clear that the Mennonite and Brethren were hesitant of having the Friends operate the program. There was also agreement that it would be desirable to have peace church funding of the program, but some argued for government subsidy of what could surely be a very expensive undertaking.[12]

In subsequent days the organization of the National Council for Religious Conscientious Objectors was further refined and developed, and on October 11 the Council was formally inaugurated. It was authorized to handle all relations between the government and conscientious objectors. The council of eight members was to have at least one member from each of the peace churches, and five additional members. M. R. Zigler was elected chairperson; Orie Miller, vice-chairperson; and Paul French, executive secretary. [13]

The creation of the council and the prominent role of a Mennonite on the council (Orie Miller) caused for the Mennonite Central Peace Committee what M. R. Zigler called a "delicate situation." In 1940 some Mennonites were as uneasy about close collaboration with the Brethren and the Friends as they were about governmental involvements. [14]

During the following week, French, Miller, Henry Fast, Paul Furnas, Homer Morris, Raymond Wilson, Zigler, and others worked strenuously to develop an alternative service plan. By October 21 a plan had been completed and presented to the National Council for Religious Conscientious Objectors for ratification.

The plan as it emerged from council discussion envisioned the creation of a National Board for Civilian Service to serve as an advisory body to an executive officer who would administer the alternative service program. The executive officer would report to the national director of the Selective Service Administration. The five-member board would be staffed by peace church members and function as an independent body after its formation.

The alternative service projects would be of two types. One would be in conjunction with government agencies and the other under direct control of peace church agencies in a variety of work camp, refugee, and relief activities both domestic and foreign.

In retrospect, the plan was an ambitious one and would have met well the high ideals and hopes of the conscientious objectors.

On October 24 Paul French delivered a nine-point memorandum to Eldridge Sibley, secretary of the Osborne committee. The newly appointed Selective Service Director, Dr. Clarence Dykstra, requested the Osborne committee to review the proposal and make recommendations to him regarding the plan.

That same day Paul French and Clarence Pickett met with Dykstra to recommend Mr. Sibley as the executive administrator of the alternative service program. From Dykstra they learned that Mr. Wayne Coy of the Osborne committee had been designated by the committee to review and revise the peace church plan.[15] The Osborne committee spent two days (October 28-29) on Coy's revision of the historic peace church plan, and on the 29th delivered a proposal to Dr. Dykstra contemplating three program options. Conscientious objectors would work in (1) government agencies; (2) camps in conjunction with government agencies, but operated by the peace churches; or (3) camps operated by the peace churches.[16]

After deliberation, the National Council for Religious Conscientious Objectors accepted the Dykstra program.

Dykstra then took the proposed program to President Roosevelt but was taken aback when the president reacted negatively to the proposal. As Paul French put it, "The president expressed instant and aggressive opposition to the plan." He also rejected the idea of conscientious objectors in civilian conservation camps, because he said that would be too easy. In fact, Roosevelt believed that all conscientious objectors should be drilled by army officers.[17]

Peace church representatives were understandably alarmed by the hostility of the president. Dykstra and French, wise to the ways of Roosevelt's Washington, enlisted the aid of one of the president's assistants and eventually the president was won over to the program.

The president's prickly attitude had a sobering effect on several dimensions of the plan, most notably on the funding of the program. Everyone involved in the program development phase had too easily assumed that funding would be secured. Colonel Hershey, in a conversation with French on October 15, had brushed aside French's concerns about funding by saying that the crucial issue was the shape of the program; the government would have to provide the funds needed.[18]

Now in December, it became clear that Selective Service Administrators Dykstra and Hershey had seriously misjudged the situation. Apparently the assumption had been that Roosevelt would actively support the program. His intense criticism made it clear that getting significant funding would be a problem.

Hence on December 5 Dykstra and Hershey met with the National Council of Religious Conscientious Objectors at a luncheon at the Hotel Harrington. With some chagrin they reported their dilemma. It became clear that the Civilian Public Service Program would have to be funded by the historic peace churches themselves. To ask for funding from Congress would be to expose the entire program to renewed hostile congressional scrutiny, which could well scuttle the entire project. Another consideration was the belated discovery by Dykstra and Hershey that any monies appropriated could legally be used solely for government-operated camps. Most members of the council were unwilling to commit to a program operated by the government.[19]

For the peace churches the awareness of the potential financial burden of Civilian Public Service was suddenly front and center. A special Standing Committee of the Church of the Brethren voted "to assume financial responsibility for training our young men, with or without government aid."[20]

The Mennonites took similar action through the Mennonite Central Committee and the Mennonite Central Peace Committee. A few Mennonites had reservations regarding the funding commitment. Wrote one: "I think we need to be real careful how we proceed, or we will find ourselves with something on our hands that we cannot handle." But the normally reserved Orie Miller more nearly represented Mennonite sentiment when he promised that Mennonites "would gladly pay their share of the bill. They would do it even though every Mennonite farmer had to mortgage his farm."[21]

For most Mennonites the private funding of the alternative service program was a highly desirable development, for it promised to allow a greater degree of autonomy for peace church control and direction. Many Friends shared this belief, reflected in a resolution by the Five Year Meeting of Friends in Richmond, Indiana, urging that government funds not be utilized even if they should become available.[22]

On December 19 Selective Service Director Dykstra presented a memorandum to President Roosevelt outlining the program known as Civilian Public Service with the argument that "there is a precedent in the successful furloughing of conscientious objectors to the Society of Friends during the World War."[23]

The president approved the plan and on February 6, 1941, signed Executive Order 8675 giving the Selective Service director authority to determine work of national importance, assign men to camps, and supervise, equip, and regulate the process.

Civilian Public Service, the program Clarence Pickett hailed as "a moral equivalent to war," was finally ratified. A unique partnership between the historic peace churches and the Selective Service System was born.

The Civilian Public Service Program Begins

When the historic peace church representatives visited President Roosevelt on January 10, 1940, neither they nor the president could have foreseen the outcome of events culminating in the president's endorsement of the Civilian Public Service design on December 20. The unprecedented passage of a draft bill in peacetime in September—more than a year before the United States declared war—surprised even the president, who continued to be uneasy about its political consequences. The strong crosscurrents generated by the interventionist-noninterventionist debate raging in the country confused even the sensitive political antennae of the president, who was in the thick of a reelection campaign when the bill finally passed Congress. As late as October 30, in his last major campaign speech when it was clear he would be reelected handily, he still felt the need to neutralize the meaning of the draft.

> And while I am talking to you mothers and fathers I give
> you one more assurance. . . . Your boys are not going to be
> sent into any foreign wars. They are going into training to

form a force so strong that, by its very existence, it will keep the threat of war far away from our shores.[24]

Conscription, according to FDR, was a weapon, not for warfare, but for diplomacy. Conscription was a manifestation of national resolve, of seriousness of purpose—a means of deterrence. This redefinition of conscription in peacetime annoyed the interventionists in 1940 who wished the president had been less categorical about the use of American manpower abroad.[25]

The unique church-state partnership, known as Civilian Public Service, enshrined in Executive Order 8675, was signed by the president on February 6, 1941. It began as a six-month experiment, but lasted through a year of uneasy peace, four years of total war, and two years of demobilization. Selective Service Director Dykstra assured the historic peace churches that the Selective Service would be prepared to ask for an appropriation if financing the program became impossible after six months.[26]

The plan assigned conscientious objectors to camps for soil conservation and reforestation work. The Agriculture and Interior Departments agreed to provide supervision for the work projects. The Federal Security Agency made civilian conservation camps available. The War Department offered dormitory furniture. Selective Service paid transportation expenses and assumed overall supervisory and policy responsibilities. The cooperating churches furnished all other necessary parts of the program including day-by-day administration of the camps, subsistence costs for the camps, and all care and maintenance of the men.

The actual relationship of the religious agencies to the Selective Service Administration was not clearly defined.

Were the churches agents of Selective Service or were they contractors, carrying out a contractual service? The answer was unclear.

The eagerness of the historic peace churches to each operate their own camps contributed to the lack of clarity. Their decision to finance their own program surely lent credence to their belief at the outset that they had nearly complete freedom to operate their own programs. They had every reason to believe that once the initial induction of their conscientious objectors was completed—the work of the local draft board—the welfare and work of the Civilian Public Service personnel would be in the hands of the churches.

Furthermore, if there were problems they had the National Service Board for Religious Objectors to turn to for assistance. Under the able leadership of Paul French, who served as its executive secretary throughout the war, the National Service Board for Religious Objectors could be the link between the camp programs and the Selective Service bureaucracy. French combined knowledge of Washington with exceptional administrative ability to create an agency which functioned with efficiency and skill.

In a general way, the National Service Board for Religious Objectors carried on liaison responsibilities with Selective Service while the church agencies—Mennonite Central Committee, American Friends Service Committee, and Brethren Service Commission—carried out the administrative functions of camp operations. In practice, nothing so simple was possible and over time the National Service Board for Religious Objectors assumed, rightfully, ever-larger spheres of responsibility.

One fundamental irony in the historic peace church effort to achieve an acceptable form of alternative service was their inability to sufficiently meld their shared religious traditions to make a closely unified program possible. Having successfully lobbied government for a service program, they were now unable to work together in that program.

The three-headed program was at times muddled, since it had to answer to three diverse organizations: the historic peace churches, the National Service Board for Religious Objectors, and the Selective Service System. There were many management difficulties, but the program could scarcely have experienced anything else given these realities.

On the other hand, the relatively decentralized structure of the program may have been a benefit, for it was a massive operation with more than one hundred and fifty camp units and many thousands of men.

Role of Selective Service

The most troublesome issue for Civilian Public Service was the role of Selective Service in the program. Clearly Selective Service was pleased with Civilian Public Service. In his December 1940 discussion of Civilian Public Service with the president, Dykstra reminded Roosevelt that "during the World War, conscientious objectors presented difficulties out of proportion to the numbers involved" and argued for Civilian Public Service as a way "to avoid so far as possible a recurrence of such difficulties."[27] He also claimed that Civilian Public Service was a cooperative experiment to see whether voluntary groups and government could work together in a great "national service."

Dykstra's successor, General Lewis Hershey, could be equally fulsome. He once called Civilian Public Service an "experiment in democracy—an experiment such as no nation has ever made before ... to find out whether our democracy is big enough to preserve minority rights in a time of national emergency."[28]

Hershey approved of Civilian Public Service, for more pragmatic reasons. When in 1943 Senator Elmer Thomas of Oklahoma introduced a bill to eliminate the conscientious objector clause, thus requiring all able-bodied men to serve in combat, Hershey argued that such a move would saddle the military with many thousands of conscientious objectors who would refuse to cooperate. It would become a nightmare for all involved. Far better, the general argued, to put them in out-of-way camps, for as he put it, "The concientious objector, by my theory, is best handled if no one hears of him."

Furthermore, the general proudly pointed out, nearly 10 percent of the conscientious objectors in Civilian Public Service are "salvaged" for military service. Besides, the conscientious objectors do work of national importance at almost no cost to the American taxpayer.[29]

The intrusion of Selective Service into Civilian Public Service operations increased as time went on. Several factors contributed to the Service's ability to exercise this increased influence: detached service in mental hospitals, the creation of government camps, and a growing number of Civilian Public Service men who were not from the historic peace churches and did not share the service orientation of alternative service. Sometimes the heavy-handed Selective Service direction gave the lie to the "civilian control" language of the conscription act.

Tom Jones, president of Fisk University and first director of Friends Civilian Public Service, recounted a trip he made to the Friends camp at Merom, Indiana, in 1941 in the company of Colonel Louis Kosch, deputy to the newly appointed director, Lewis Hershey.

As Jones spoke enthusiastically about what he hoped could be accomplished through Civilian Public Service, Colonel Kosch interrupted him with "Who do you think you are? Don't you know I'm in charge of these camps under Selective Service?"

Jones replied that he thought the historic peace churches were promised complete autonomy.

"My dear man," said Kosch, "the draft is under United States government operation. Conscientious objectors are draftees just as soldiers are. Their activities are responsible to the government. The peace churches are only camp managers."[30]

This incident early in the Civilian Public Service period set the tone in terms of the Selective Service Administration's understanding of the program. It never varied thereafter. The famous memo of Lieutenant Colonel McLean in late 1942 encapsuled the Selective Service view perfectly. Said McLean,

> The program is not being carried on for the education of an individual, to train groups for foreign service or future activities in the postwar period, or for the furtherance of any particular movement. Assignees can no more expect choice of location or job than can men in the Service. . . . From the time an assignee reports to camp until he is finally released he is under the control of the Director of Selective Service. He ceases to be a free agent and is accountable for all of his time, in camp and out, 24 hours a day. His movements, ac-

tions, and conduct are subject to control and regulation. He ceases to have certain rights and is granted privileges. These privileges can be restricted or withdrawn without his consent as punishment, during emergency, or as a matter of policy. He may be told when and how to work, what to wear, and where to sleep. He can be required to submit to medical examinations and treatment, and to practice rules of health and sanitation. He may be moved from place to place and from job to job, even to foreign countries, for the convenience of the government regardless of his personal feelings or desires.[31]

In the fall of 1940 the founders of Civilian Public Service would have found such a comprehensive statement of control unacceptable. But by the end of 1942 they were too deeply committed to demand a redefinition. For many of the Civilian Public Service men—particularly the educated and the conscientious objectors who were not from one of the historic peace churches—McLean's statement confirmed their experience and fueled their discontent with Civilian Public Service.

Civilian Public Service Issues

The first Civilian Public Service camp (Friends) opened at Patapsco State Park near Baltimore on May 15, 1941. During the next months numerous other camps were opened. By March 1942, about 3000 men were part of the Civilian Public Service system.

"Detached service," or noncamp work, began in June 1942 with the assignment of men to a mental hospital in Elgin, Illinois. That effort had to be abruptly terminated a few months later because of community opposition to the conscientious objector presence. But by then other mental hospital projects were begun. Eventually about one-fifth of all Civilian Public Service men were in mental hospital work.

By 1944 probably the majority of men were serving in some form of "detached service," including such interesting projects as Florida hookworm eradication projects, forest fire "smoke-jumping" units in the far West, and service as "guinea pigs" for health-related experiments at the National Institutes of Health. An imaginative plan to open service units for conscientious objectors in China was grounded with the passage of the Starnes Act in 1943 which prohibited conscientious objectors from serving beyond the continental United States. Thus even though many Civilian Public Service men continued to serve in camps, many options were available to them and many availed themselves of those alternative assignments.

In terms of camp administration, the Mennonites fared best. Their men came from a tradition which assumed a high degree of church authority, so camp administration was simply an extension of such practice for most of them. Both their farm orientation and their nonresistant theology made it easy for them to accept relatively mundane work. The key point for them was to be free from participation in war. It was less important to be actively resisting the war and its evils.

The Brethren and especially the Friends had far greater diversity among their men in terms of opinion and practice. A concerted effort was made to operate along democratic lines. Kitchen work, recreation, worship, and even work projects in some camps were carried on by general consensus.

For many of the men, the type of work most camps afforded—such as wood cutting, ditch digging, setting fence posts, and other manual labor in out-of-way places—was unrewarding and frustrating. This was especially true in the Brethren and Friends camps, and for those who sought to express their conscientious objection by humanitarian service or active resistance to the war effort. Not only did such work fail to use their abilities and training, but it was hard to see how such work could have much redeeming social value.

General Hershey's dictum—that the conscientious objector is "best handled if no one hears of him"—was quite literally their experience. The frustration of such men, combined with the growing manpower shortages in American welfare institutions and the painful financial pressures of operating the camps, provided an incentive to move toward detached service.

Mental hospital work met the desire of many men for more specifically humanitarian work, but even this work was not without its problems. Conscientious objectors found terrible conditions in most mental hospitals. Their efforts to improve conditions nearly always led to conflict with administrators with all the attending publicity such matters generated. Such events were particularly distressing to the Selective Service. Nevertheless, the mental hospital work did bring improvements in many institutions.

Selective Service, despite much self-serving rhetoric, never advanced beyond seeing Civilian Public Service as a semipunitive program for conscientious objectors who would otherwise give everyone a lot of trouble. The camps remained the center of the program throughout the war.

Improvements were made, however. More frequent visitors, more democratic procedures, and more funds for education were all evidence of progress. The Brethren tried specialized camps, one being a fine arts camp at Waldport, Oregon, which produced literary materials. The Friends operated an orientation camp at Big Flats, New York, for incoming conscientious objectors.[32]

The absence of pay for work and inadequate dependency support was a serious matter of grievance for some men, especially among those conscientious objectors who were not from the historic peace churches. During the second year of the war, more than a thousand Civilian Public Service men signed a petition requesting pay, challenging the right of the government and the churches to make them work for no pay. Both the historic peace churches and Selective Service were fearful that a request for pay would result in a congressional reaction inimical to conscientious objectors and the Civilian Public Service program.

In retrospect it is clear their fears were well founded. Civilian Public Service had almost no friends in Congress during World War II. In fact, it had many enemies. Given the president's thinly veiled hostility to the program, opening the matter for review might well have led to disaster. Furthermore the historic peace churches—particularly the Brethren and Mennonites—were genuinely convinced that the no-pay proviso demonstrated the seriousness of conviction of their conscientious objectors.

However, for some of the men the pay and governance issues were a matter of conviction. In the course of the war more than 200 men walked out of the camps and into prison, preferring prison to compromises they found unacceptable in Civilian Public Service.

When Civilian Public Service was established, government-operated camps represented one of three possible forms of the program, but the historic peace church desire to operate their own camps made the government camps unnecessary.

The presence of nonhistoric peace church conscientious objectors in church camps, however, led to growing discontent. In 1943 the Methodist Church, which had the third largest numer of conscientious objectors in Civilian Public Service (after the Mennonites and Brethren), took the lead in demanding the creation of government camps. The first camp was set up at Mancos, California, in July 1943. Several other camps were opened later. Unfortunately, the camps became one means Selective Service could use to discipline conscientious objectors who created trouble. Neither the churches nor the courts had been of much help to Selective Service when Civilian Public Service men used the Civilian Public Service system to express their convictions against conscription.

Whether by design or not, the government camps filled up with the least cooperative, most politically conscious campers. The government camps also became the setting for those whose philosophy of conscientious objection gave high credence to resistance to war. The camps became arenas setting for action against conscription by imaginative noncooperation. Those who lacked sympathy for the alternative service philosophy of Civilian Public Service now had a way to put their convictions to work against Selective Service.

The result was a long ordeal of frustration for all involved. The lesson of government camps was not lost on the historic peace churches. When the 1948 conscription program was developed, one alternative they quickly rejected was government management of camps.

When Civilian Public Service was conceived in the fall and winter of 1940, the historic peace churches and Selective Service found general agreement on a number of issues:

> 1. Conscientious objectors would not oppose the war while it was being fought.
> 2. Conscientious objectors would demonstrate their sincerity by making significant sacrifices, such as eschewing pay for work.
> 3. Conscientious objectors would cause as little trouble as possible.
> 4. Conscientious objectors should not be overly visible. Rather, they should work in camps in out-of-way places.
> 5. Conscientious objectors should be kept out of the army and, as far as possible, out of jail.
> 6. The historic peace churches should operate alternative service (Civilian Public Service), administratively and financially.

Civilian Public Service illustrated the possibilities as well as the ambiguities of alternative service in the modern total-war society. Once the government recognized the appropriateness of alternative service for conscientious objectors, the design of the program came reasonably close to satisfying all parties involved. The historic peace churches genuinely wanted to pay their own way. Doing so gave them greater autonomy to operate their own camps. Equally important, it validated their loyalty to the country and their seriousness of purpose. They were making serious sacrifices for the sake of their convictions. Conscientious objection had to be sacrificial to be the moral equivalent to war. Furthermore the program provided an outlet for humanitarian service.

The government was pleased. The conscientious objector was a practical nuisance, but the Civilian Public Service program provided a means to solve the problem with minimum effort. Political fallout—which terrified politicians and bureaucrats—was neutralized by the arrangement. Thoughtful public opinion was satisfied by the financial sacrifice and by the camp setting. It wasn't prison, but its imagery had a benevolent penal quality.

CHAPTER 6

Alternative Service and the Cold War

"Might it not be in everyone's best interest to simply put all conscientious objectors in jail?"
—Representative Paul Shafer
(R-Mich.), 1951

The Draft Act, 1948

President Truman announced the "Truman Doctrine" in March 1947. He offered economic and military help to nations menaced by armed minorities or outside aggression.

By 1947 the "iron curtain" described by Winston Churchill a year earlier began to take shape. Truman rushed aid to Greece and Turkey. In June 1947 George Marshall announced the Marshall Plan, committing massive American economic assistance for European recovery efforts.

In response the Soviets created the Central European "Cominform" and the sovietization of Eastern Europe proceeded apace. A communist coup d'etat in February

1948 in Czechoslovakia sent tremors of alarm through the halls of Congress and the State Department.

On March 17, 1948, just a year after the Selective Service Act of 1940 ended, Truman called for the reinstatement of the draft. It was time, Truman believed, for the American people to demonstrate their resolve in the face of Soviet aggression. Secretary of State George Marshall testified on behalf of a new draft law. He argued that diplomatic action "without the backing of military strength in the present world can only lead to appeasement."[1]

Dr. Karl Compton, president of the Massachusetts Institute of Technology and chair of the president's Advisory Committee on Universal Military Training, made a similar point. Implementing a draft "will be a deterrent to action by any nation which might provoke war, as it would have been a powerful deterrent against Hitler, Mussolini, and Japan.[2] Of course, Compton forgot that the 1940 draft act had been enacted a year before the United States entered the war and had no perceptible effect on the behavior of any of the combatants.

Congress held hearings on the new military training bill during April and May 1948. The historic peace churches actively opposed the resumption of conscription. The Friends were particularly concerned that a stress on conscientious objector provisions might dissipate their protest of universal military training. Said the American Friends Service executive committee:

> We ought not to let the concern for conscientious objector provisions interfere with opposition to conscription or draft bills of any kind. It was also felt that there should be no implication that we would take part in administering any conscription law.[3]

The Senate version of the bill was nearly identical to the 1940 Draft Act. It afforded conscientious objectors who refused noncombatant service an opportunity to do "work of national importance under immediate civilian direction." The only change was a clause providing workman's compensation in the event of disablement or death.[4]

Harold Bender testified on behalf of Mennonite Central Committee Peace Section, arguing for four refinements in the conscientious objector provisions:

1. Exempt absolutist conscientious objectors completely.

2. Make the alternative service program entirely civilian, with no military personnel involved.

3. Give complete control of the service program for their conscientious objectors to the respective church agencies.

4. Require the government to provide maintenance allowances and wages for all men in the program.[5]

Bender's four points were a distillation of experience in two world wars. It was a good summary of the preferred historic peace church alternative service program.

Conscientious Objector Deferment

When the bill came to the floor of the Senate, Senator Wayne Morse (R-Oreg.) introduced an amendment which the historic peace churches had helped frame. The senator confessed his lack of sympathy for conscientious objectors, but he believed that religious freedom and the lessons of Word War II required a change in government policy toward the conscientious objector. "We cannot have religious freedom under the constitution and then in practice deny it to those who seek to exercise it."[6]

The Morse Amendment proposed the creation of a National Commission on Conscientious Objectors composed of civilians appointed by the president to:

> prescribe the condition under which persons claiming conscientious objection shall a) be inducted into the armed forces, b) be assigned to noncombatant service, c) be assigned to service of national importance of approved private agencies operating in the public good at home or abroad; or d) be deferred.[7]

The board would hear all appeals and have authority to prescribe all administrative rules and regulations including pay and dependency allowances. The Morse plan for the board was an almost exact replica of the English Tribunals of World War II which had worked so well in England.

Morse's amendment was defeated by a vote of 48 to 22. Senator Gurney, chair of the Senate Armed Services Committee, summarized the sentiment of the majority: "The way the conscientious objectors were taken care of during the war worked out very well generally."[8]

The conscientious objector provision in the House bill caught the historic peace churches by surprise. It called for simple, complete deferment for the conscientious objector.

How such a liberal step could have emerged is not clear. Previous Congresses had always rejected simple deferment out-of-hand. The only source of information is Ora Huston, executive secretary for the National Service Board for Religious Objectors. Huston reported that Chairperson Walter Andrews (R-N.Y.), during a closed session of the Armed Services Committee, inquired of Secretary of Defense Forrestal whether he objected to deferring conscientious objectors rather than putting them in "concentration camps." Forrestal replied that he had no objection, and the committee decided to adopt deferment.[9] Equally surprising, there was no debate about the matter on the House floor.

The historic peace churches were delighted. Selective Service Director Hershey was not. He was sure, he told the members of Congress, that if the government did not require conscientious objectors to perform "some work in accord with their religious beliefs," while other men served in the military, there would be a public protest. "The history of America and of other countries is that whenever you establish a means of being deferred or being exempted from service, many there are who develop the specifications necessary to qualify."[10]

Against all odds the deferment proviso survived the Senate-House Conference Committee deliberations. The Conference Report on the compromise bill which emerged, observes that the Senate "receded from its disagreement" with the House bill. It agreed to accept wording on the disposition of conscientious objectors identical to that in the House version.[11]

When he presented the conference report to the Senate, Senator Gurney merely remarked, "With respect to the conscientious objectors the Senate yielded to the House. Those who oppose any military service . . . are deferred and are not put in conscientious objector camps."[12]

How could such a thing have happened? Ora Huston of the National Service Board for Religious Objectors speculated that "in the give and take of compromise the House conscientious objector provision may have been accepted because so many other provisions of the bill were unacceptable to the Conference committee." [13]

President Truman signed the bill on June 24. The Selective Service Act of 1948 was law. In the annals of conscientious objection to war it was historic. Deferment rather than alternative service was the lot of conscientious objectors.

This nearly flawless solution for conscientious objectors suffered one major shortcoming, however. It contained a new qualification for conscientious objector status. The 1940 act defined the conscientious objector as one who "by religious training and belief, is opposed to participation in war in any form." The 1948 law added the proviso that religious training and belief meant "belief in relation to a Supreme Being involving duties superior to those arising from any human relation." It ruled out "essentially political, sociological, or philosophical views or a merely personal moral code."

During the spring as the bill was being written, the historic peace churches had tried to expand the definition. They wanted to include "religious training and belief or humanitarian conviction."[14] However, Congress rejected that idea for a more restrictive definition. Why? During the world war local draft boards had diverged widely in interpreting the meaning of religious training and belief. Congress intended the more specific definition to correct that deficiency and provide more specific criteria for draft board decisions. A more immediate concern was a desire to eliminate the political conscientious objector. In 1948 Congress meant to thwart socialists and communists who might take advantage of a loose definition to evade military service.[15]

The historic peace churches were ambivalent about the

new law. They could hardly believe their good fortune in the deferment clause, but they were chagrined by the "Supreme Being" proviso. A. J. Muste was outraged. He called on all religious people to "repudiate utterly this injustice and refuse any action which may involve acquiescence in this provision and collaboration in its administration."[16]

The complaints were not heeded, however, and a court test in *George v. United States* in 1952 failed.[17] Not until *U.S. v. Seeger* in 1965, when the Supreme Court defined "religious training and belief" in such broad terms as to make "Supreme Being" a nullity was the definition discarded.[18]

The practical effect of the new definition was that on the one hand local draft boards fell back on historic peace church membership as a basic criteria. On the other hand, nonreligious conscientious objectors found themselves virtually without recourse. Justice Department Appeals hearing officers by and large gave a strict interpretation to the law. By April 1949 the Justice Department had sentenced and imprisoned nearly 40 men, with many more at various stages of appeal.[19]

Deferment or Service?

The 1948 act was to have run for five years, but a successful amendment by Wayne Morse reduced it to two years. Thus in early 1950, Congress again turned its attention to draft issues. On June 30, 1950, five days after the North Koreans crossed into South Korea, Truman signed the Selective Service Extension Act. The draft was to continue to July 9, 1951.[20]

By July 1950 American troops were in battle and in September the Inchon invasion began. In November the Americans were badly mauled by the Chinese. As Congress began work on military manpower needs in early 1951, it was apparent that the country was in a tough war. Monthly draft calls rose from 20,000 in September to 80,000 in March 1951. By September 1951 total inductions reached 700,000 men.[21]

Coupled with the growing draft calls were rising casualty lists. *News Notes* observed that those normally antagonistic to conscientious objectors were becoming more vocal. *Newsweek* reported that "since the outbreak of hostilities in Korea, many families with sons overseas have complained vociferously about the lenient treatment given to objectors."[22] Selective Service, always edgy about public sentiment, reported that in several communities, local citizens had painted the barns of conscientious objectors and had "treated [them] shamefully in public places."[23]

In Montana deferred Hutterites were the focus of hostility. In Pondera County the entire draft board resigned in protest in January 1951. The board declared:

> It is our considered judgment that no young man regardless of his religious beliefs should be relieved of serving in either combat or non-combatant units in defense of his country in which he makes his livelihood and by virtue of whose constitution he enjoys many freedoms.... We believe such service is the duty of every young man, regardless of color, race or creed...."[24]

The State legislature took up the cause with a bill declaring "military noncooperation" a crime. Another bill denied state office holding to all conscientious objectors. Neither bill passed, but the legislature did dispatch to Washington a memorial signed by the governor demanding that Congress cut out the deferral clause from the draft law. A former Civilian Public Service man from Missoula, observing the commotion, believed the replacement of alternative service for deferment would relieve most of the discontent.[25]

By December 1950 Ray Wilson of the Friends Committee on National Legislation in Washington was predicting that even though "General Hershey ... has repeatedly said he doesn't want the headache the job involves, the Civilian Public Service program will be revived within the near future." Rumors even had it that Selective Service was quietly recruiting World War II staff in preparation for a Civilian Public Service-like plan it was ready to present to Congress.[26]

Christian Century magazine urged the historic peace churches to begin thinking about the nature of a new alternative service.

> Church sponsorship of Civilian Public Service camps in World War II turned into a dubious and expensive headache. The element of compulsion which was inextricably involved, defeated the best efforts of church leaders to develop work for social and civic betterment. . . . So the task which the churches now face will not be an easy one. But that is greater reason for getting on with it.[27]

The National Service Board for Religious Objectors Consultative Council met in January 1951 in Baltimore. The forty participants represented seventeen denominations. Everyone agreed on the desirability of continuing deferment. That not being possible they then developed a six-point basis for a return to alternative service.

The program should (1) be civilian administered; (2) offer more than government assignments; (3) include church and privately organized projects or individual assignments; (4) provide remuneration for work; (5) limit term of service to that of the military; and (6) offer complete exemption for absolutists.[28]

The American Friends Service Committee, building on those conditions, created a statement entitled "Guiding Principles for Consideration in the Event of Passage of Legislation Calling for Service for Conscientious Objectors." The Friends added a seventh point; that any work "should be of national importance including service of international significance in the United States and abroad."[29] They had in mind physical and mental health services, scientific experimentation, and agricultural and technical assistance to developing countries. The Friends wanted no more "leaf-raking" jobs if they could help it.

Congress was in a hurry to get draft legislation on the books. Lyndon Johnson (D-Tex.), chair of the Preparedness Subcommittee of the Senate Armed Services Committee, claimed it was a time of "national emergency" with the country "on the threshold of full mobilization."[30] In the rush to get increased draft levies and a universal military training program into the draft law, the Defense Department (whose staff drafted the amendments) may have overlooked conscientious objector issues. However, the peace church spokespersons raised the issue in their testimony to the Senate Armed Service Committee.

After Harold Bender concluded his remarks to the committee, Senator Saltonstall (R-Mass.) queried whether the

Department of Defense had dealt with the conscientious objector. Lyndon Johnson replied that they had not. Later, after testimony by Norman Thomas, Paul Shafer (R-Mich.) thanked Thomas for reminding him of the conscientious objector matter and inquired whether it might not be in everyone's best interest to simply put all conscientious objectors in jail.[31]

The House Armed Services Committee did discuss the issue, but persistent historic peace church lobbying of the members led to retention of conscientious objector deferment. The Senate committee, however, proposed alternative service and a determined effort by historic peace church representatives to get the language changed to deferment failed. The Senate bill required "work of national importance under civilian direction"—the language of 1940.

The change from deferment to alternative service happened after the hearings closed, and was apparently the work of the Senate Armed Services drafting committee, ratified during an executive session of the committee. In any case, Senator Wayne Morse protested the change, which he claimed was not discussed in the hearings nor by the full committee.[32]

The historic peace churches asked Morse to help get the deferment clause back in the bill, but he demurred. They then approached Senator Sparkman (D-Ala.) with the idea of keeping deferment as an option, but creating a National Commission on the Conscientious Objector to determine disposition of those opting for alternative service. Sparkman agreed to talk to Senator Russell, chairman of the Armed Services Committee, but nothing came of the effort.[33]

By early May 1951, the House and Senate passed their respective bills. The House retained deferment; the Senate called for alternative service. The Conference Committee of Representatives and Senators now became the focus of historic peace church efforts. Aware that they would almost certainly lose deferment, they asked for several changes in the alternative program. They hoped to move alternative service more directly toward social service. So they proposed a change from "work of national importance under civilian direction" to "work of national health, safety, and interest." They also proposed that boards not place conscientious objectors directly in jobs. Rather, they should merely suggest broad categories which the president would define.[34]

The historic peace church lobbying was so persistent it began to irk committee members. George Loft of the American Friends Service Committee described his last-minute meeting with representative Dewey Short.

> Short was very sharp in saying proponents for the conscientious objectors were asking too much and had pushed him too hard. He had had his ears pinned back in the conference committee on the matter of occupational appeal, and he was not at all inclined to mention it again. He described the possibility of allowing conscientious objectors to volunteer with service agencies as giving them sanctuary.... [I] tried to explain the reasons for these suggestions, but the discussion was decidedly strained.[35]

One matter of particular concern to representatives of Congress was the possibility that boards would continue to defer those who were contributing to national health and safety. Senator Mike Mansfield reflected the sentiment of his colleagues when he spoke at length against the possibility that a Mennonite farmer be allowed to stay on his father's farm to help with necessary food production. He said conscientious objectors should

> at least be required to do work that is definitely in the national interest and not merely improving their pocketbooks. . . . These people, like the rest of the population, should sacrifice their normal activities to some extent in the interest so that they would not be avoiding all national service.[36]

A New Alternative Service

Congress adopted the Conference report on May 29, 1951. It amended the Selective Service Act of 1948 by

> striking out in the third sentence thereof [section 6c] the words be deferred and inserting in lieu thereof the following: in lieu such induction [the conscientious objector shall] be ordered by his local board, subject to such regulations as the President may prescribe, to perform for a period prescribed in section 4 (b) [24 months] such civilian work contributing to the maintenance of the national health, safety and interest as the local board may deem appropriate.[37]

The Korean war had destroyed deferment. Alternative service was the law. The form of alternative service was yet to be designed.

There was surprising agreement. No one but the most hawkish representatives wanted camps. When queried on the matter, Senator Richard Russell, chair of the Armed

Services Committee, responded, "I do not know that the language would specifically prevent assignment of conscientious objectors to camps. However, I would be less than frank if I did not state that it was the intention of the conferees not to have camps of that nature established on a national scale."[38]

The Selective Service System was extremely reluctant to reenact Civilian Public Service. In May it became apparent that an alternative service program would replace deferment. A Selective Service administrator told the historic peace churches that Selective Service was trying to get rid of the assignment by moving it to another department. But "nobody wants the hot potato," he said.[39]

The historic peace churches agreed that they would not again serve as government agents, administering prescribed assignments over which they had little control. The Friends were especially adamant on the point. The day after Congress passed the bill, Lewis Hoskins, executive secretary of the American Friends Service Committee, sent a letter to Arthur Fleming, head of the Manpower Policy Commission. He declared that Friends would "make no blanket agreement to execute or enforce regulations governing conscientious objectors drawn up by outside agencies."[40]

Congress assigned Selective Service the task of developing the new program. The National Service Board for Religious Objectors cautioned its constituents that the new program would emerge slowly. As it turned out, it was more than a year before the new system began to function. In the meantime, deferment remained in effect.

The historic peace churches now turned the focus of attention to Selective Service. The Selective Service System was under terrific pressure to develop a new set of regulations governing universal military training for armed forces personnel. The revised classification system replaced the old IV-E designation for conscientious objectors with I-O (conscientious objector available for civilian work) and I-W (conscientious objector performing civilian work).

In late fall Selective Service finally began work on the conscientious objector program. Not until February 20, 1952, did President Truman sign Executive Order 10238 prescribing the shape and form of the new program.[41] It was not all the historic peace church had hoped for, but it was an improvement on Civilian Public Service.

Christian Century commented that the new regulations were

> much better than those in force during the previous war. They insure that the conscientious objector will do work of real national, international, and social importance. They do not involve churches in the ambiguous responsibilities they assumed while conducting the Civilian Public Service program.[42]

When Stauffer Curry met with the National Service Board for Religious Objectors board in early March, he was enthusiastic. He said, "We are met at what may prove to be the beginning of a new era in the history of conscientious objection to military training and service."[43]

Conscientious objectors would work in government or nonprofit organizations engaged in charitable, health welfare, education, and scientific work. They would not work in agencies for profit nor remain in their own communities, except in special cases. They could volunteer, choose their service job, or even serve abroad.

State Selective Service directors were responsible for the immediate supervision of the program. Finding approved jobs became their responsibility. The program was ready to begin.

Then came the bombshell. Congress refused to appropriate funds for the alternative service program. Selective Service had requested $150,000. The House Appropriations Committee, in a bad mood, granted $15,000. The bewildered Selective Service staff finally concluded that they didn't need a special appropriation. They could use Selective Service general funds for the program.[44]

Almost immediately a new problem loomed ahead: Where to find the estimated 5,000 conscientious objector jobs in a tight labor market? As early as February, Colonel Kosch and Victor Olson of Selective Service reported that their search for jobs had been futile. Job scarcity, budget constraints, civil service regulations, and unions conspired to make job placement of conscientious objectors a major headache.[45]

Would the historic peace churches help? The Mennonites offered immediate help. The National Service Board for Religious Objectors also decided to help. Stauffer Curry said, "It seems somewhat obvious that the success of the present conscientious objector program will depend to a considerable extent upon the resourcefulness of interested groups and persons in discovering significant work opportunities."[46]

Soon the National Service Board for Religious Objectors accepted an invitation to coordinate responsibility for all employment opportunities in private nonprofit agencies. This made the Friends very uneasy.

In April 1952, more than 20 Yearly Meeting representatives met at Evanston. Several weeks later, the American Friends Service Committee board met with General Hershey. As a result of these meetings, the Friends decided tentatively to cooperate, subject to a final definition of the arrangement.[47]

However, when they met with Hershey in July to work out final details, the Friends discovered significant restrictions by Selective Service. All units and projects required state Selective Service director approval before placements could be made. Already Brethren Service Commission projects in California and Texas had been rejected. The American Friends Service Committee also learned that Selective Service intended to retain control over I-Ws. They wanted to reserve the right to transfer them whenever their presence created "public relations problems." Hershey was blunt in saying that any group participating in the conscientious objector program was acting as an agent of Selective Service.[48]

The American Friends Service Committee board met on September 17. After "long and prayerful searching," it concluded it could not participate in the program. Lewis Hoskin wrote to General Hershey, explaining the decision.

> Our experience in Civilian Public Service showed us that it would be impossible to maintain our philosophy of service if we were again to assume an administrative position under a draft agency.[49]

Thomas Botts expressed well the Friends' position.

> The Mennonite and Brethren attitude is different from that of the Friends. They are willing to work with any programs that will allow them to keep control of their own

conscientious objectors, and they are willing to adhere to Selective Service regulations because of this. Our position is more of opposition for military purposes, and of unwillingness to be a party to the success of the conscription operation.[50]

The Brethren and Mennonites consigned some control over conscientious objectors to Selective Service. The trade-off was their ability to guide their young men into programs and projects the churches believed important and which would nourish their spiritual growth. The alternative would have been to settle for jobs designed by Selective Service. These would not, of course, have had the altruistic and spiritual goals in focus. Thus a compromise was necessary.

The Friends were no longer convinced of the appropriateness of alternative service in the context of the modern warfare state. In fact they now saw conscientious objection as a means to challenge war and conscription.

The I-W Program

The I-W program began operating officially in July 1952. The initial shortage of jobs improved by late 1952.

A wide variety of service opportunities became available to draftees. A number of farmers were assigned to the American Dairy Herd Improvement Association and to Agricultural Department experimental farms. Brethren Service arranged opportunities in relief and welfare work in a number of European settings. Mennonites created PAX service, which employed conscientious objectors around the world in construction, agricultural development, and relief activities. A group of men served as "guinea pigs" at the National Institutes of Health at Bethesda, Maryland.[51]

Most I-Ws accepted low-level jobs in health facilities. In fact, I-W became nearly synonymous with hospital work, since so many conscientious objectors engaged in such jobs. By 1954 more than 80 percent of all I-Ws held hospital jobs.[52]

By the summer of 1953 Selective Service had approved more than 1,200 institutions and agencies for I-W assignments. Over 3,000 men were enrolled.[53] Most of them were from farm and rural communities. For many, the new environments and vocations had life-changing consequences. A conscientious objector at Staten Island Hospital observed:

> Most of us I-Ws have made or are making the greatest and most radical occupational change of our lives. . . . Nearly all of us here are farm boys who suddenly and almost unexpectedly were ushered into an entirely new way of livelihood.[54]

Said another:

> Working in a mental hospital has been a new experience to all of us and it has opened our eyes to the needs of the mentally ill and to the sinful and lost condition of the world.[55]

For many, the experience shaped their lives toward "caring" professions, often leading to more education. Of course not all experienced these benefits. For some it was a dreary, boring detour. The men enjoyed greater freedom with little of the regimen and enforced discipline of Civilian Public Service. Unit activities were often established where groups of I-Ws were clustered.

Of the nearly 10,000 I-Ws from 1952 to 1955, only about 25 men left their jobs without authorization. Of that number about 20 were Jehovah's Witnesses who were uneasy about the I-W program at their induction.[56]

Overall, the Mennonites and Brethren were quite happy with the program. Conscientious objectors volunteered for service rather than waiting for induction, illustrating the appeal of the program. There were other reasons for this appeal. Pay for work was a factor. Most jobs were interesting. Many were challenging and altruistic.

Furthermore, the term of service was fixed. A demoralizing aspect of Civilian Public Service had been the "duration of war" time frame. The I-W program gave the young men what most of them sought: an opportunity to serve God and perform humanitarian work instead of military service but within a defined time frame.

But there were problems as well. The men sometimes melted into their settings without any special witness about who they were or what they stood for. The ease of entry into the program and the short duration of service limited the sense of sacrifice evoked by the Civilian Public Service program. Since many assignments were individual in nature, support groups were often nonexistent. Membership attrition from the churches in the course of I-W service was substantial.

Summing Up

A satisfactory alternative service emerged only after persistent and strenuous effort. It offered a form of witness against war. It also offered a positive outlet for civic responsibility agreeable to politicians, soldiers, and the public.

Alternative service has proven least acceptable in times of war when military sacrifices are high and the war is popular. In the state of suspended war during much of the 1950s and 1960s, public demand for equivalent service or sacrifice became less vociferous.

One attractive feature of alternative service was its charming ability to meet two basically contradictory needs at the same time. For the historic peace church conscientious objectors, humanitarian and altruistic work met deeply held needs nourished by centuries of religious history and practice. That moral ground also met the public and political demands for sacrifice by conscientious objectors who refused to participate in the American military system.

The most desirable option was complete deferment from all obligation for service. This was not possible, except for a three-year period during a fit of Congressional carelessness. That option quickly disappeared in the context of the Korean War with its high casualties and large draft calls.

The story just told is in some sense a modus vivendi—a temporary arrangement based on particular circumstances and a particular era in our national history. If historic peace church convictions move from a service orientation to a resistance-to-war conviction, the arrangements achieved by 1955 may not continue to be possible.

The central lesson of this story is the accommodation of interests between the historic peace churches and the military system. However, in that accommodation several other gains developed. One was the growing sophistication of the historic peace churches in influencing the Washington bureaucracy. They learned how to use influence politics skillfully. The M. R. Ziglers, Orie Millers, Paul Frenches, Ray Wilsons, and others learned to walk the corridors of power. They learned to make the contacts which counted when important issues were at stake.

On the Selective Service side, especially in the legislative arena, precedents are all-important. The Civilian Public Service experience in World War II was a major element contributing to the advances achieved in the I-W program. In influence politics, the ability to cite prior experience or practice is all-important.

Of course, the fortunate appointment of General Lewis Hershey as director of Selective Service contributed to the outcome. It is easy to be critical of the general's forked-tongue messages. Indeed, he often said one thing to congressional critics or American Legion fanatics and another to the historic peace churches. However, in the process he made the fragile arrangements work.

He was the man in the middle and best exemplifies the accommodations thesis. To him the key reality was the conscientious objector nuisance factor. His first concern was to reduce the nuisance factor to a minimum. This was surely helpful to the historic peace churches. When the Civilian Public Service camps encountered certain problems, Hershey was ready to accede to a new plan such as the I-W program.

The contrasting intractable stance of his understudy, Colonel Kosch, shows how important Hershey was in this evolution. Despite Kosch's disastrous experience with government Civilian Public Service camps, he was ready to try them again. He was lukewarm about the I-W program. Had Kosch been in Hershey's place, the story of alternative service might have been quite different.[57]

During this four-decade period, the Brethren and Mennonites continued almost unchanged in their commitment to alternative service. By 1950 the Friends, on the other hand, had shifted their focus from alternative service to resistance to war. The evolution of that change is a complex shift in convictions and experience.

Rufus Jones' exasperated protest to W. J. Swigart in the spring of 1918 was a harbinger of the Friends' convictions in the 1950s. "It apparently did not occur to the Washington people," wrote Jones, "that our objection was anything more than an objection of the direct killing of people. They do not seem to understand that we are opposed to the military system . . . ."[58]

The American Friends Service Committee concern for the absolutist conscientious objector during preparation to visit Roosevelt in early 1940 reflected the Quaker concern to witness against war. It signaled the growing uneasiness of at least some Friends with alternative service. By 1950 the Friends were convinced that the role of the conscientious objector must be to resist the war system directly. They made it a matter of policy.

The drive for alternative service for conscientious objectors was a remarkably sustained and focused effort. The historic peace churches had no political leverage. Their constituencies were among the most single-mindedly nonpolitical, nonparticipatory groups in American society. They had few votes. What they did have was a moral and religious conviction embodied in practice. The successful evolution of the I-W program was a direct legacy of the travail and fortitude of the historic peace church conscientious objectors of World War I and World War II.

Notes

Chapter One

1. Roland Bainton, *Christian Attitudes Toward War and Peace* (Nashville, 1960), p. 79.
2. C. J. Cadoux, *The Early Christian Attitude to War* (London, 1919), p. 17. See also Jean-Michel Hornus, *It Is Not Lawful for Me to Fight* (Scottdale, 1980).
3. Paul Gia Russo, "The Conscientious Objector in American Law," *Religion in Life*, Summer, 1941, pp. 333-334.
4. Ibid.
5. Guy Hershberger, *War, Peace, and Nonresistance* (Scottdale, 1944), pp. 98-106.
6. Samuel L. Horst, *Mennonites in the Confederacy: A Study of Civil War Pacifism* (Scottdale, 1967), p. 80.
7. *The Friend*, August 10, 1916, p. 80.
8. "A Documentary Record of the Formation and Operations of the Haverford Emergency Unit, 1917," Book II, Haverford College Library.
9. Elizabeth Grey Vining, *Friend of Life: A Biography of Rufus M. Jones* (Philadelphia, 1958), p. 158.
10. Ibid.
11. Rufus Jones, *A Service of Love in Wartime* (New York, 1920), pp. 10-11.
12. Ibid.
13. Ibid., p. 50.

Chapter Two

1. Blanche Cooke, *Wilson and the Anti-Militarists* (Ph.D. dissertation, Johns Hopkins University Press, 1970), pp. 78-79.
2. David A. Lockmiller, *Enoch H. Crowder: Soldier, Lawyer and Statesman* (Columbia, Missouri, 1955), p. 152.
3. Daniel R. Beaver, *Newton D. Baker and the American War Effort, 1917-1919* (Lincoln, Nebraska, 1966), p. 33.
4. Public Law No. 12, 65th Congress, 1st Session (Washington: 1917).

5. Guy F. Hershberger, *War, Peace, and Nonresistance* (Scottdale, Pennsylvania, 1944), p. 116.

6. Cooke, p. 203.

7. Ibid., p. 310.

8. Ibid., p. 204.

9. Beaver, p. 231.

10. Cooke, p. 210.

11. *Conscientious Objection*, Special Monograph No. 11, Volume I (Washington, 1950), p. 55.

12. Charles Chatfield, *For Peace and Justice: Pacifism in America, 1914-1941* (Knoxville, Tennessee), p. 70.

13. Baker to Wilson, May 26, 1917, Baker Papers.

14. Donald Johnson, *The Challenge to American Freedoms* (University of Kentucky Press, 1963), p. 17.

15. Beaver, pp. 33-34.

16. Cooke, p. 214.

17. *The Friend*, June 21, 1917, pp. 616-617.

18. Oral Interview, Orie O. Miller, March 4, 1972, Stoltzfus notes, file 237.

19. C. E. Boyer to W. J. Swigert, November 5, 1917, Sappington notes.

20. D. A. Crist to W. J. Swigart, October 25, 1917, Sappington notes.

21. *American Friend*, September 6, 1917, p. 712.

22. Ibid.

23. Griest to Crowder, July 2, 1917, Griest Papers.

24. Griest to Wilson, August 27, 1917, Griest papers.

25. Ibid.

26. Griest to W. J. Swigart, August 28, 1917, Griest Papers.

27. Report, August 22, 1917, Executive Committee, American Friends Service Committee Archives.

28. *Gospel Herald*, September 1, 1917, p. 409.

29. *Friends Intelligencer*, September 1, 1917, p. 553.

30. *Conscientious Objection*, Special Monograph No. 11, Volume I, p. 58.

31. Ibid., pp. 58-59.

32. Quoted by Frederick Palmer, *Newton D. Baker: America At War.* Volume I (New York, 1931), p. 341.

33. Beaver, p. 232.

34. Ibid.

35. Ibid.

36. Senate Report, No. 202, 65th Congress, 2d Session.

37. Wilson to H. C. Early, February 12, 1918, quoted in *Gospel Messenger*, March 2, 1918, 136.

38. Peace Committee Minutes, March 22, 1918, American Friends Service Committee Archives.

39. Ibid., March 23, 1918.

40. Executive Committee Minutes, April 1, 1918, American Friends Service Committee Archives.

41. Ibid., April 4, 1918.

42. *New York Times,* June 2, 1918.

43. Jones to Swigart, May 31, 1918, File 29, Stoltzfus File.

44. "Statement Authorized by the War Department and Text for the Order of the Secretary in Reference to Conscientious Objectors," May 30, 1918 (War Department, Washington, D.C., 1918).

45. Jones to Swigart, May 31, 1918, American Friends Service Committee Archives.

46. Rufus M. Jones, *A Service of Love in Wartime* (New York, 1920), p. 113.

Chapter Three

1. Loucks to Swigart, February 3, 1920, Central Service Committee, Mennonite file, Box 2, Brethren Historical Library and Archives.

2. Early to Swigart, April 7, 1920, Central Service Committee, Box 1, Brethren Historical Library and Archives.

3. J. S. Hartzler, *Mennonites in the World War* (Scottdale, Pa., 1921), pp. 226-227.

4. *The Peace Testimony of the Society of Friends,* "The International Service of the Society of Friends," Commission VII (London, 1920), p. 8.

5. Ibid., "The Relation of the Society of Friends to the Peace Testimony," Commission V (London, 1920), p. 10.

6. Ibid., "Education: The Road To Peace," Commission IV (London, 1920), p. 41.

7. Melvin Gingerich, *Service for Peace* (Mennonite Central Committee, Akron, Pa., 1949), p. 18.

8. Ibid., p. 21.

9. Sources for Mennonite Forestry Services are Jacob Sudermann, "The Origin of Mennonite State Service in Russia, 1870-1880," *Mennonite Quarterly Review,* XVII (January 1943), pp. 23-46. See also Abraham Gorz, *Ein Beitrag zur Geschichte des Forstdienstes der Mennoniten in Russland* (Lenzmann, 1906).

10. See Rufus M. Jones, *A Service of Love in Wartime* (New York, 1920).

11. Clarence E. Picket, *For More Than Bread* (Boston, 1953), pp. 339-340.

12. Gingerich, pp. 25-26.

13. Roger Sappington, *Brethren Social Policy, 1908-1958* (Elgin, 1961), p. 63.

14. Rufus Bowman, *The Church of the Brethren and War* (Elgin, 1944), p. 252. See also pp. 242-243.

15. Guy F. Hershberger, "The Committee on Peace and Social Concerns and Its Predecessors," Unpublished paper, 1966, File 52, Stoltzfus Papers, p. 7.

16. Ibid.

17. Krehbiel to Miller, June 26, 1935; Keim to Krehbiel, September 24, 1935; Balderston to Krehbiel, July 15, 1935, Folder 140, Mennonite Library and Archives.

18. Wood to Krehbiel, July 5, 1935, Folder 140, Mennonite Library and Archives.

19. "Register of Participants," Folder 22, Mennonite Library and Archives.

20. "Preliminary Statement," Folder 141, Mennonite Library and Archives.

21. "Minutes of the Joint Committee of the Historic Peace Churches,"

Chicago, February 18, 1936. Brethren Peace Program file, Brethren Historical Library and Archives.

22. Guy F. Hershberger, *The Mennonite Church in the Second World War* (Scottdale, 1951), pp. 251-252.

23. Charles Chatfield, *For Peace and Justice: Pacifism in America, 1914-1941* (Knoxville, 1971), pp. 266-281.

24. Sappington, pp. 74-75.

25. Pickett to Zigler, December 24, 1936, AFSC file, 1932-1937, Brethren Historical Library and Archives.

26. Sappington, p. 75.

27. Reich to Zigler, May 28, 1939, Sappington notes.

28. Sappington, p. 78.

29. Guy F. Hershberger, "Is Alternative Service Desirable and Possible?" *Mennonite Quarterly Review*, 9 (January 1935), p. 33.

30. Ibid.

31. Sappington, p. 73.

32. Ibid. See also Bowman, pp. 258-262.

33. Gingerich, p. 27; Bowman, p. 274.

34. Pickett, p. 309.

35. Miller to Diener, September 8, 1939. PPC file, 15-3. Mennonite Archives.

36. Sappington, p. 198.

37. Random notes, 37-16. Hiebert file, Mennonite Library and Archives.

38. Gingerich, pp. 35, 43.

39. Bender to Harshbarger, October 26, 1939, 34-2 Harshbarger file 15. Mennonite Library and Archives.

40. Balderston to Wilson, November 1, 1939. Peace Section files, American Friends Service Committee.

41. Wilson to Bender, December 7, 1939, 34-2, Harshbarger file 16, Mennonite Library and Archives.

42. Bender to Balderston and Bowman, December 18, 1939, 34-2, Harshbarger file 16, Mennonite Library and Archives.

43. Balderston to Wilson, December 21, 1939, 34-2, Harshbarger file 16, Mennonite Library and Archives.

44. Wilson to Balderston, December 26, 1939, 34-2, Harshbarger file 16, Mennonite Library and Archives.

45. Miller to Bender, December 29, 1939, 34-2, Harshbarger file 16, Mennonite Library and Archives.

46. Balderston to Wilson, January 1, 1940, 34-2, Harshbarger file 16, Mennonite Library and Archives.

47. Bowman, p. 255.

48. Hiebert to Harshbarger, January 13, 1940. 43-2, Harshbarger file 16, Mennonite Library and Archives.

Chapter Four

1. Gingerich, p. 36.

2. The words E. L. Harshbarger used in a letter to Bohn, April 11, 1940, Sap-

pington notes, file 15, Mennonite Library and Archives.

3. Zigler to Picket, April 11, 1940, Sappington notes, file 15, Sappington, p. 86.

4. Earlham College Conference Report, July 2-4, 1940, American Friends Service Committee Archives.

5. Samuel R. Spencer, Jr., "A History of the Selective Training and Service Act of 1940 from Inception to Enactment." Ph.D. Dissertation. Harvard University, 1951, p. 101.

6. Ibid., pp. 74, 76.

7. Ibid., p. 80.

8. Grenville Clark to Morris Sheppard, June 22, 1940. Box 116. National Archives.

9. J. Garry Clifford and Samuel R. Spencer. Jr.. *The First Peacetime Draft* (Lawrence, Kans., 1986), p. 24.

10. Ibid., pp. 27, 70.

11. Ibid., p. 48.

12. Ibid., pp. 50-51.

13. Mark Lincoln Chadwin, *The Warhawks: American Interventionists Before Pearl Harbor* (New York, 1968), p. 29.

14. Clifford and Spencer, p. 71.

15. Ibid., p. 77.

16. Wadsworth to Wendell Willkie, July 24, 1940. Wadsworth Papers, Box 21, Series 3-c, Library of Congress.

17. Clifford and Spencer, p. 83.

18. Ibid.

19. Chadwin, p. 29.

20. Clifford and Spencer, p. 110.

21. Ibid.

22. Hearings on S. 4164 before the Senate Committee on Military Affairs, 73d Congress, 3d Session (Washington, 1940), p. 3.

23. Miller to Sheppard, July 12, 1940, File 413. Mennonite Archives.

24. Paul Comly French, *We Won't Murder* (New York, 1940), p. 175.

25. Wilson to Wychoff, March 25, 1941, Peace Section file, American Friends Service Committee Archives. Sibley and Jacob, pp. 47-48.

26. Paul Comly French Diary, July 25, 1940. Swarthmore College Peace Collection.

27. Ibid.

28. Ibid., August 7, 1940.

29. Ibid., August 27, 1940.

30. Ibid., September 7, 1940.

31. Ibid., September 12, 1940.

32. Guy Hershberger Papers, September 13, 1940. Box 38. Mennonite Archives.

33. RG/47, Box 29, File 110, Selective Service Archives.

34. Miller to Newton, August 13, 1940. File 16-3. Mennonite Archives.

35. Zigler to Skiles, August 2, 1940, Sappington Notes.

Chapter Five
1. Spencer, pp. 409, 443; French Diary, August 27, 1940, Swarthmore College Peace Collection.
2. *Conscientious Objection*, Special Monograph No. 11, Vol. 1 (Selective Service System, 1950), p. 86.
3. Guy Hershberger collection, Minutes, Box 38, Mennonite Archives.
4. French diary, September 11, 13, and 17, 1940. Swarthmore College Peace Collection.
5. French memo to War Problems Committee, September 18, 1940, file 24/1, Peace Problems Committee, Mennonite Archives.
6. Fast to Harshbarger, September 19, 1940, Harshbarger Correspondence, 34-2, file 20, Mennonite Library and Archives.
7. Oral interview with J. N. Weaver, October 14, 1973, File 75, Stoltzfus papers, Eastern Mennonite College Archives.
8. French to War Problems Committee, October 2, 1940, Orie Miller files, 16-4, Mennonite Archives.
9. War Problems Committee Minutes, October 4, 1940, Swarthmore College Peace Collection.
10. West to French, September 29, 1940. Sappington notes.
11. French diary, October 5, 1940, Swarthmore College Peace Collection.
12. Bowman, p. 293.
13. Gingerich, pp. 55-56.
14. Zigler to Morris, October 8, 1940, Sappington notes.
15. Pickett journal, October 24, 1940.
16. *Origins of Civilian Public Service* (Washington, NSBRO), p. 6.
17. Ibid., French to Pickett, December 3, 1940, p. 21.
18. War Problems Committee, October 15, 1940, Swarthmore College Peace Collection.
19. Minutes, December 23, 1940, Fellowship of Reconciliation Papers, Box 2, Swarthmore College Peace Collection.
20. *Origins of Civilian Public Service*, pp. 7-8.
21. Brunk to Miller, December 13, 1940, file 12/4, Mennonite Archives. Pickett, *For More Than Bread*, p. 324.
22. Ibid., p. 319.
23. *Origins of Civilian Public Service*, p. 25.
24. The *New York Times*, October 31, 1940.
25. Chadwick, p. 130.
26. NSBRO, Minutes, December 10, 1940, Swarthmore College Peace Collection.
27. Mulford Q. Sibley and Philip E. Jacob, *Conscription of Conscience* (Ithaca, 1952), p. 122.
28. Ibid., p. 123.
29. *Congress Looks at the Conscientious Objector* (Washington, NSBRO, 1943), pp. 56, 61.
30. Tom Jones, *Light on the Horizon* (Richmond, Indiana, 1961), p. 142.
31. "Statement of Policy, Camp Operations Division of the Selective Service

System," 1942, in Sibley and Jacob, p. 509.
  32. *Conscientious Objector*, VIII, March 1946, pp. 3, 6.

Chapter Six
  1. *Report of the Director*, Office of Selective Service Records, p. 94. See also *Hearings*, Senate Armed Services Committee, 1948, p. 4.
  2. *Hearings*, Committee on Armed Services, House, Eightieth Congress, Second Session, HR 6274 and HR 6401, April 12—May 3, 1948, pp. 326-327.
  3. American Friends Service Committee Executive Committee minutes, May 25, 1948, American Friends Service Committee files.
  4. *Congressional Record*, Eightieth Congress, Second Session, 94, 7, June 15, 1948, to June 19, 1948, p. 9267.
  5. Statement on "Conscription for Military Training, and Provisions for Conscientious Objectors," submitted to the president's Advisory Commission on Universal Military Training, April 10, 1948. Bender used this document for his Senate hearing testimony.
  6. *Congressional Record*, Eightieth Congress, Second Session, 94, 6, June 3, 1948, p. 7277.
  7. Ibid., p. 1778.
  8. Ibid., p. 7305.
  9. National Service Board for Religious Objectors Consultative Council Minutes, June 29, 1948, p. 2.
  10. *Hearings*, House Armed Services Committee, June 1948, pp. 1613-1614.
  11. *House Miscellaneous Reports*, Eightieth Congress, Second Session, 5, No. 2438, pp. 1, 10.
  12. *Congressional Record*, Senate, June 1948, p. 8996.
  13. National Service Board for Religious Objectors Consultative Council Minutes, June 29, 1948, Swarthmore College Peace Collection, p. 2.
  14. *The Reporter*, October 1948, p. 2.
  15. Ibid., p. 3.
  16. Muste, *Five Point Statement*, presented to National Service Board for Religious Objectors Consultative Council, June 29, 1948; Wittner, *Rebels Against War*, p. 186.
  17. George v. United States, 196F. 2nd 445. cert. denied, 344, U.S. 843 (1952).
  18. Arlo Tatum and Joseph S. Tuchinsky, *Guide to the Draft* (Boston, 1970), p. 180. See also John C. Osberger, "Three Eras of the Conscientious Objector," *University of Cincinnati Law Review*, 34 (Fall, 1965), p. 497.
  19. Michael Harrington, "Politics, Morality and Selective Dissent" in Finn, *A Conflict of Loyalties*, p. 221. See also *News Notes*, CCCO files, Swarthmore College Peace Collection, p. 2.
  20. Lewis Hershey, *Outline of Historical Background of Selective Service and Chronology* (Washington, Government Printing Office, 1952), pp. 19-21.
  21. Ibid., Table 3, pp. 38-40.
  22. *News Notes*, January 1951, p. 4. "Calling up COs," *Newsweek* XL, 5 (August 4, 1952), p. 77.
  23. Memorandum on informal discussion with General Renfrew, Colonel

Kosch, and Colonel Griffing of Selective Service, National Service Board for Religious Objectors Directors minutes, June 11, 1951, Addendum A, Swarthmore College Peace Collection, p. 5; A. Stauffer Curry to Board of Directors, National Service Board for Religious Objectors, May 22, 1951, American Friends Service Committee files, p. 2.

24. *Religious News Service*, January 2, 1951, National Service Board for Religious Objectors files, Swarthmore College Peace Collection, p. 6.

25. *The Reporter*, April 16, 1951, p. 5.

26. *Religious News Service*, December 29, 1950. See also December 19, 1950.

27. *Christian Century*, LXVII, 38 (September 20, 1950), p. 1092.

28. National Service Board for Religious Objectors, Consultative Council Minutes, January 1951, Swarthmore College Peace Collection.

29. "Guiding Principles...." March 26, 1951, American Friends Service Committee Archives.

30. *Hearings*, Preparedness Subcommittee, Committee on Armed Services, United States Senate, Eighty-Second Congress, First Session on S. 1, Universal Military Service and Training Bill . . . January 10-February 2, 1951, p. 24.

31. Ibid., p. 982.

32. Ray Wilson memo, March 14, 1951, American Friends Service Committee files.

33. Ibid.

34. Memo on "Conscientious Objector Provisions in the Proposed UMTS Bill Now Being Considered by the House-Senate-Conference Committee," May 24, 1951, American Friends Service Committee files.

35. *CO Services Historical Report #2*, American Friends Service Committee Activities Re CO Clause in 1951 Draft Act, George Loft, July 1951, American Friends Service Committee files.

36. *Congressional Record*, House, June 7, 1951, p. 6260.

37. *Conference Report* (House Report. N. a535), Congressional Record, House, Eighty-Second Congress, First Session, 97, June 7, 1951, p. 6247.

38. *Congressional Record*, Senate, Eighty-Second Congress, First Session, 97, 4, June 1, 1951, pp. 6026-6027.

39. National Service Board for Religious Objectors Directors minutes, May 1951, Addendum B, National Service Board for Religious Objectors files, Swarthmore College Peace Collection, p. 5.

40. Lewis Hoskins to Dr. Arthur Fleming, June 20, 1951, American Friends Service Committee files, p. 2.

41. *The Reporter*, January-February, 1952, pp. 1-2.

42. *Christian Century*, March 5, 1952, pp. 268-269.

43. National Service Board for Religious Objectors Directors-Consultative Council Minutes, March 5-6, 1952, Addendum A, National Service Board for Religious Objectors files, p. 1.

44. *News Notes*, March-April 1952, p. 1.

45. Memo, "Interview with Kosch and Olson," February 25, 1952, National Service Board for Religious Objectors files, Swarthmore College Peace Collection, p. 1.

46. National Service Board for Religious Objectors Directors-Consultative Council Minutes, March 5-6, 1952, Addendum A, National Service Board for Religious Objectors files, Swarthmore College Peace Collection, p. 3.

47. George Loft to Stauffer Curry, April 15, 1952, National Service Board for Religious Objectors files, Swarthmore College Peace Collection. See also *News Notes,* June 1952, p. 1.

48. George Loft, memo, "Meeting with General Hershey," July 29, 1952, American Friends Service Committee files, pp. 1-2.

49. Hoskins to Hershey, September 18, 1952, American Friends Service Committee files, p. 1.

50. American Friends Service Committee Board meeting minutes, September 17, 1952, American Friends Service Committee files, p. 1.

51. *The Reporter,* June 1954, pp. 1-2.

52. *I-W Mirror,* July 28, 1954, p. 2.

53. *News Notes,* September 1953, p. 3.

54. *The Coastal Compass,* June 1955. p. 1.

55. Ibid., July 1955, p. 2.

56. *Conscientious Objector,* Work Program, n.d. National Service Board for Religious Objectors files, SCPC. 2; National Service Board for Religious Objectors Consultative Council Minutes, March 31, 1955. Addendum H, National Service Board for Religious Objectors files, Swarthmore College Peace Collection.

57. French diary, July 11-12, 1946, Swarthmore College Peace Collection.

58. Jones to Swigart, May 31, 1918. file 29, Stoltzfus file.

Bibliography

I. Manuscript Collections

American Friends Committee Archives (Philadelphia, Pa.)
    Civilian Public Service Papers
    Executive Committee Minutes
    Peace Section Papers
Anonymous, *The Draft* (New York: Hill and Wang, 1968).
Army War College Archives (Carlisle, Pa.)
    General Lewis B. Hershey Papers
Brethren Historical Library and Archives (Elgin, Ill.)
    Brethren Service Committee Papers
Haverford College Library (Haverford, Pa.)
    Haverford Emergency Unit Papers
    Rufus Jones Papers
Library of Congress
    Newton D. Baker Papers
Menno Simons Historical Library and Archives (Eastern Mennonite College, Harrisonburg, Va.)
    Grant Stoltzfus Papers
Mennonite Archives (Goshen, Ind.)
    Civilian Public Service Records
    Mennonite Central Committee Papers
    Mennonite Peace Problems Committee Papers
Mennonite Historical Library and Archives (Bethel College, Kans.)
    World War I Oral History Collection
Selective Service Archives (Washington, D.C.)

Swarthmore College Peace Collection (Swarthmore, Pa.)
Fellowship of Reconciliation Papers
Friends War Problems Committee Papers
National Service Board for Religious Objectors Records
Paul C. French Diary

II. Books

Abrams, Roy H., *Preachers Present Arms* (Philadelphia: Round Table Press, Inc., 1933).

An Introduction to Friends Civilian Public Service (Philadelphia: American Friends Service Committee, 1945).

Anonymous, *The Draft* (New York: Hill and Wang, 1968).

Backer, Rachel, *Conscience, Government and War: Conscientious Objection in Great Britain 1939-1945.* (London: Routledge and Kegan, Paul, 1982).

Bainton, Roland H., *Christian Attitudes Toward War and Peace* (New York: Abingdon Press, 1960).

Baskis, Lawrence M., and William A. Strauss, *Chance and Circumstance: The Draft, the War and the Vietnam Generation* (New York: Knopf, 1978).

Beaver, Daniel R., *Newton D. Baker and the American War Effort, 1917-1919* (Lincoln: Nebraska Press, 1966).

Benjamin, Philip S., *The Philadelphia Quakers in the Industrial Age, 1865-1920* (Philadelphia: Temple University Press, 1976).

Bowman, Rufus D., *The Church of the Brethren and War, 1708-1941* (Elgin, Ill.: Brethren Publishing House, 1944).

Brinton, Howard H., *Sources of Quaker Peace Testimony* (Wallingford, Pa.: Pendle Hill Historical Studies, 1942).

Brock, Peter, *Pacifism in Europe to 1919* (Princeton: Princeton University Press, 1972).

Brock, Peter, *Pacifism in the United States: From the Colonial Period to the First World War* (Princeton: Princeton University Press, 1969).

Brock, Peter, *Twentieth-Century Pacifism* (New York: Van Nostrad Reinhold, 1970).

Brooks, Arle and Robert J. Leach, *Help Wanted: The Experience of Some Quaker Conscientious Objectors* (Wallingford, Pa.: Pendle Hill Press, 1940).

Cadoux, C. J., *The Early Christian Attitude to War* (London: Headley Bros., Publishers, Ltd., 1919).

Chadwin, Mark Lincoln, *The Warhawks: American Interventionists Before Pearl Harbor* (New York: W. W. Norton, 1968).

Chatfield, Charles, *For Peace and Justice: Pacifism in America, 1914-1941* (Knoxville: University of Tennessee Press, 1971).

Clifford, J. Garry, and Samuel R. Spencer, Jr., The First Peacetime Draft (Lawrence, Kans.; University Press of Kansas, 1986).

Congress Looks at the Conscientious Objector (Washington: National Service Board for Religious Objectors, 1943).

Conscience and War: A Report on the Treatment of Conscientious Objectors in World War II (New York: American Civil Liberties Union, 1943).

Conscientious Objection, Special Monograph No. 11, Vol. 1 (Washington: Selective Service System, 1950).

The Conscientious Objector Under the Selective Training and Service Act of 1940 (Washington: National Service Board for Religious Objectors, 1942).

Cornel, Julian, *Conscience and the State: Legal and Administrative Problems of Conscientious Objectors, 1943-1944* (New York: John Day Company, 1944).

Cornel, Julian, *The Conscientious Objector and the Law* (New York: John Day Company, 1943).

Crowder, E., *The Spirit of Selective Service* (New York: The Century Company, 1920).

Daniels, Josephus, *The Wilson Era: Years of War and After, 1917-1923* (Chapel Hill, North Carolina: University of North Carolina Press, 1946).

Davies, A. Tegla, *Friends Ambulance Unit: The Story of the FAV in the Second World War, 1939-1946* (London: George Allen and Union Ltd., 1947).

Detweiler, Richard C., *Mennonite Statements on Peace, 1915-1966* (Scottdale, Pa.: Herald Press, 1969).

Directory of Civilian Public Service (Washington: National Service Board for Religious Objectors, 1947).

Duggan, J. C., *Legislative and Statutory Development of the Federal Concept of Conscription for Military Service* (Washington, D.C.: The Catholic University of America Press, 1946).

Durnbaugh, Donald F., *European Origins of the Brethren* (Elgin, Ill.: Brethren Press, 1958).

Durnbaugh, Donald F., ed., *To Serve the Present Age* (Elgin, Ill.: Brethren Press, 1975).

Eisan, Leslie, *Pathways of Peace* (Elgin, Ill.: Brethren Publishing House, 1948).

The Experience of the American Friends Service Committee in Civilian Public Service (Philadelphia: American Friends Service Committee: 1945).

Fellowship of Reconciliation, *Why America Should Not Adopt Conscription* (Philadelphia: American Friends Service Committee, 1940).

Finn, James, *A Conflict of Loyalties: The Case for Selective Conscientious Objection* (New York: Pegasus, 1968).

Forbes, John, *The Quaker Star Under Seven Flags, 1917-1927* (Philadelphia: University of Pennsylvania Press, 1962).

French, Paul C., *We Won't Murder* (New York: Hastings House, 1940).

Fry, A. Ruth, *A Quaker Adventure* (London: Friends Service Council, 1943).

Gingerich, Melvin, *Service for Peace* (Akron, Pa.: Mennonite Central Committee, 1949).

Hamilton, Wallace, *Clash by Night* (Wallingford, Pa.: Pendle Hill, 1945).

Handbook for Conscientious Objectors (Philadelphia: Central Committee for Conscientious Objectors, 1952).

Hartzler, J. S., *Mennonites in the World War* (Scottdale, Pa.: Mennonite Publishing House, 1921).

Hassler, R. Alfred, *Conscripts of Conscience* (New York: Fellowship of Reconciliation, 1942).

Hayes, Denis, *Conscription Conflict* (London: Sheppard Press, 1949).

Hentoff, Nat, *Peace Agitator: The Story of A. J. Muste* (New York: Macmillan Company, 1963).

Hershberger, Guy Franklin, *The Mennonite Church in the Second War* (Scottdale, Pa.: Mennonite Publishing House, 1951).

Hershberger, Guy Franklin, *War, Peace, and Nonresistance* (Scottdale, Pa.: Herald Press, 1944).

Hershey, Lewis B., *Outline of Historical Background of Selective Service and Chronology* (Washington: Government Printing Office, 1952).

Horsch, John, *The Principle of Nonresistance as Held by the Mennonite Church* (Scottdale, Pa.: Mennonite Publishing House, 1927).

Horst, Samuel L., *Mennonites in the Confederacy* (Scottdale, Pa.: Herald Press, 1967).

Jacobs, Clyde E., and John F. Gallagher, *The Selective Service Act: A Case Study in the Governmental Process* (New York: Dodd, Mead and Company, 1967).

Jacobs, Philip E., *Origins of Civilian Public Service* (Washington: National Service Board for Religious Objectors, 1946).

Jannaway, F. G., *Without the Camp: Being the Story of Why and How the Christadelphians Were Exempted from Military Service* (London, privately published, 1917).

Johnson, Donald, *The Challenge to American Freedom: World War I and the American Civil Liberties Union* (Lexington: University of Kentucky Press, 1963).

Jones, Mary Hoxie, *Swords into Ploughshares: An Account of the American Friends Service Committee, 1917-1937* (New York: Macmillan Company, 1937).

Jones, Rufus, M., *A Service of Love in Wartime* (New York: Macmillan Company, 1920).

Jones, Thomas, *Light on the Horizon* (Richmond, Ind.: Friends United Press, 1961).

Juhnke, James C., *A People of Two Kingdoms: The Political Acculturation of the Kansas Mennonites* (Newton, Kansas: Faith and Life Press, 1972).

Kellogg, Walter Guest, *The Conscientious Objector* (New York:

164   Politics of Conscience

Boni and Liveright, 1919).

Klippenstein, Lawrence, ed., *That There Be Peace: Mennonites in Canada and World War II* (Winnipeg: Manitoba Conscientious Objectors Reunion Committee, 1979).

Krehbiel, H. P., *War-Peace-Amity* (Newton, Kans.: Herald Publishing Company, 1937).

Larson, Zelle Andrews, *An Unbroken Witness: Conscientious Objection to War, 1949-1953* (Ph.D. dissertation, University of Hawaii, 1975).

Leach, Jack Franklin, *Conscription in the U.S.: Historical Background* (Rutland, Vt.: Tuttle Publ. Co., 1952).

Lew, Daniel H., *A History of the Selective Training and Service Act of 1940* (Ph.D. dissertation, Harvard University, 1941).

Lingemans, Richard R., *Don't You Know There's a War On? The American Home Front, 1941-1945* (New York: Putman, 1970).

Lockmiller, David A., *Enoch H. Crowder: Soldier, Lawyer, and Statesman* (Columbia: University of Missouri Studies, 1955).

Lukas, Sidney, ed., *The Quaker Message* (Wallingford, Pa.: Pendle Hill, 1948).

Lynd, Staughton, ed., *Nonviolence in America: A Documentary History* (New York: Bobbs, Merrill Company, Inc., 1966).

MacMaster, Richard K. with Samuel L. Horst and Robert F. Ulle, *Conscience in Crisis: Mennonites and Other Peace Churches in America, 1739-1789* (Scottdale, Pa.: Herald Press, 1979).

Markmann, Charles Lam, *The Noblest Cry: A History of the American Civil Liberties Union* (New York: St. Martin's Press, 1965).

Millis, Walter, *Arms and Men: A Study in American Military History* (New York: G. P. Putman, 1956).

Mooney, Chase C., and Mildred E. Layman, "Some Phases of the Compulsory Training Movement, 1914-1921, *Mississippi Valley Historical Review*, XXVIII (March 1952), pp. 633-656.

Nelson, John K., *The Peace Prophets: American Pacifist Thought, 1919-1941* (Chapel Hill, North Carolina: Uni-

University Caroline Press, 1967).

Niebanck, Richard J., *Conscience, War, and the Selective Objectors* (New York: Lutheran Church in America, 1968).

The Non-Cooperator and the Draft (Philadelphia: Central Committee for Conscientious Objectors, 1963).

Olmstead, Frank, *They Asked for a Hard Job: CO's at Work in Mental Hospitals* (New York: Plowshare Press, 1943).

Pacifist Handbook: Questions and Answers Concerning the Pacifist in Wartime, Prepared as a Basis for Study and Discussion (Philadelphia: American Friends Service Committee, 1939).

Palmer, Frederick, *Newton Baker* (New York: Dodd, Mead & Company, 1931).

Peace, War and Military Service: A Statement of the Position of the Mennonite Church (Scottdale, Pa.: Mennonite Publishing House, 1937).

Peacetime Conscription: A Problem for Americans (Philadelphia: American Friends Service Committee, 1944).

Peterson, H. C. and Gilbert C. Fite, *Opponents of War, 1917-1918* (Madison: University of Wisconsin Press, 1957).

Pickett, Clarence E., *For More Than Bread* (Boston: Little, Brown and Company, 1953).

Rae, John, *Conscience and Politics: The British Government and the Conscientious Objector to Military Service, 1916-1919* (London: Oxford University Press, 1970).

The Right to Refuse to Kill: A New Guide to Conscientious Objection and Service Refusal (Geneva: International Peace Bureau, 1917).

Rohr, John Anthony, *Prophets Without Honor: Public Policy and the Selective Conscientious Objector* (Nashville: Abingdon Press, 1971).

Rohrer, Peter Lester, and Mary E. Rohrer, *The Story of the Lancaster County Conference Mennonites in Civilian Public Service, with Directory* (Smoketown, Pa.: nd. 1946).

Roop, John D., *Christianity vs. War* (Ashland, Ohio: Brethren Publishing Company, 1949).

Sappington, Roger E., *Brethren Social Policy, 1908-1958* (Elgin, Ill.: The Brethren Press, 1961).

Scheiber, Harry, *The Wilson Administration and Civil Liberties* (Ithaca: Cornel University Press, 1960).

Schlissel, Lillian, ed., *Conscience in America* (New York: E. P. Dutton and Company, 1968).

Sibley, Mulford Q., and Ada Wardlaw, *Conscientious Objectors in Prison, 1940-1947* (Philadelphia: Pacifist Research Bureau, 1945).

Sibley, Mulford Q. and Philip E. Jacob, *Conscription of Conscience: The American State and the Conscientious Objector, 1940-1947* (Ithaca: Cornel University Press, 1952).

Spencer, Samuel R., "A History of the Selective Training and Service Act of 1940 from Inception to Enactment" (Ph.D. dissertation, Harvard University, 1951).

Springer, Keith, James Juhnke, and John D. Waltner, *Voices Against War: A Guide to the Showalter Oral History Collection on World War I Conscientious Objection* (North Newton, Kans.: Bethel College Historical Library and Archives, 1973).

Statements of Religious Bodies on the Conscientious Objector (Washington National Service Board for Religious Objectors, 1968).

Tatum, Arlo and Joseph S. Tuchinsky, *Guide to the Draft* (Boston: Beacon Press, 1970).

Tatum, Lyle, ed., *The Peace Testimony of Friends in the 20th Century* (Philadelphia: Friends Coordinating Committee on Peace, 1965).

Thomas, Evan W., *Why We Oppose Military Conscription* (New York: War Resistors League, 1944).

Thomas, Norman, *The Conscientious Objector in America* (New York: B. W. Huebsch, Inc., 1923).

Unruh, John D. *In the Name of Christ: A History of Mennonite Central Committee and Its Service, 1921-1951* (Scottdale, Pa.: Herald Press, 1952).

Vining, Elizabeth Gray, *Friend of Life: The Biography of Rufus M. Jones* (Philadelphia: J. B. Lippincott and Company, 1958).

Wagler, David, and Roman Raber, *The Story of the Amish in Ci-*

vilian Public Service (North Newton, Kans.: Bethel Press, 1945).

Weisbord, Marvin R., *Some Form of Peace* (New York: Viking Press, 1968).

West, Dan, *What Ought a Conscript Do* (Elgin, Ill.: Brethren Service Committee, 1940).

What About the Conscientious Objector? (Philadelphia: American Friends Service Committee, 1940).

Why We Refused to Register (New York: Fellowship of Reconciliation, 1941).

Wilson, E. Raymond, *Thus Far on My Journey* (Richmond, Ind.: Friends United Press, 1976).

Wilson, E. Raymond, *Uphill for Peace: Quaker Impact on Congress* (Richmond, Ind.: Friends United Press, 1975).

Witte, William S., *Quaker Pacifism in the United States, 1919-1942* (Ph.D. dissertation, Columbia University, 1954).

Yoder, Edward, *Compromise with War* (Akron, Pa.: Mennonite Central Committee, 1944).

Yoder, Edward and Don Smucker, *The Christian and Conscription—An Inquiry Designed as a Preface to Action* (Akron, Pa.: Mennonite Central Committee, 1945).

Zahn, Gordon C., *Another Part of the War: The Camp Simon Story* (Amherst: University of Massachusetts Press, 1979).

Zahn, Gordon C., *War, Conscience and Dissent* (New York: Hawthorn Books, Inc., 1967).

III. Articles and Periodicals

"A Plan of Wartime Procedure," *Fellowship*, II (April 1936), p. 7.

Albrecht, Paul, "Civilian Public Service Evaluated by Civilian Public Service Men" *Mennonite Quarterly Review* XXII (January 1948).

Baldwin, R. N., "Conscience Under the Draft," *Nation*, 153 (August 9, 1941), pp. 114-116.

Bender, Harold S. and Jesse W. Hoover, "The War Bond Campaign," *Gospel Herald* XXXVI (September 23, 1943), p. 528.

Boisen, Anton T., "Conscientious Objectors: Their Morale in Church-Operated Service Units," *Psychiatry*, VII (May 1944), pp. 215-224.

Bourne, Randolph, "A Moral Equivalent for Universal Military Service," *The New Republic*, VII (July 1, 1916), pp. 217-219.

Bowie, W. R., "Some Choose Jail Rather Than Register: Eight Students of Union Theological Seminary," *Living Age*, 359 (December 1940), pp. 330-333.

Bueckert, Johann P., "A Chapter from Alternative Service in Russia," *Mennonite Quarterly Review* XXII (April 1948), pp. 132-135.

Chamberlain, W. H., "American Conscientious Objectors: Wartime Handling of the Small Minority Who Refuse to Fight, A Test of Freedom of Conscience," *Survey Graphic*, 32 (November 1943), pp. 436-440.

"The C.P.S. Strikes," Politics, III (July 1946), pp. 177-180.

"The Conscientious Objector," *Gospel Herald* XXXVI (August 26, 1943), p. 451.

Crespi, Leo P., "Attitudes Toward Conscientious Objectors and Some of Their Psychological Correlates," *Journal of Psychology*, XVIII (1944) pp. 81-117.

Crespi, Leo P., "Public Opinion Toward Conscientious Objectors," *Journal of Psychology*, XIX (1945), pp. 209-310.

Dahlke, H. Otto, "Values and Group Behaviour in Two Camps for Conscientious Objectors," *American Journal of Sociology*, VI (July 1945), pp. 22-33.

Drange, E. R., "Reminiscences of War Experiences" *Gospel Herald* XXVII (March 21, 1935), p. 1087.

Frankenberg, Lloyd, "Conscience Free" *Harpers Magazine* (1947).

"The Future of the C. O. Camps," *Christian Century*, LX (September 22, 1943), pp. 1063-1065.

Gaeddert, Albert, "What We Have Learned from Civilian Public Service," *Mennonite Life* I (July 1946), pp. 16-20.

Geiger, Henry, and Gordon Cough, "Origins of CPS: Another View," *Fellowship* (September 1946).

"Germfask C. O.'s Say *Time* Missed Real Story," *Fellowship*, XI (April 1945), p. 65.

Gory, Adrian E., and David C. McClelland, "Characteristics of Conscientious Objectors in World War II," *Journal of Consulting Psychology*, XI (September-October, 1947), pp. 245-257.

Hershberger, Guy, "Is Alternative Service Desirable and Possible?" *Mennonite Quarterly Review* IX (January 1935), pp. 20-37.

Hostetter, C. N., "Spiritual Significance of Civilian Public Service," *Gospel Herald* XXXIV (March 19, 1942), p. 1090.

Juhnke, James, "Mennonites and the Great Compromise," *The Mennonite* (September 23, 1969).

Kaufmann, Milo, "The Chicago C.P.S. and Relief Conference," *Gospel Herald* XXXIV (November 20, 1941), pp. 722-723.

Kepler, Ray, "An Open Letter to CPS Men," *Politics*, II (June 1945), pp. 167-168.

Kreider, Robert, "The Historic Peace Churches Meeting in 1935," *Mennonite Life*, June 1976).

Masland, John W., "Treatment of the Conscientious Objector Under the Selective Service Act of 1940," *American Political Science Review*, XXXVI (August 1942), pp. 697-701.

"Mennonite Central Committee, 1920-1970," *Mennonite Quarterly Review*, XLIV (July 1970), pp. 213-340.

Metzler, Edgar, "Is Alternate Service a Witness for Peace?" *Gospel Herald* (December 11, 1962).

Russo, Paul Gia, "The Conscientious Objector in American Law," *Religion in Life*, X (Summer, 1941), pp. 333-345.

Snyder, John M., "On the Civilian Bond Question," *Gospel Herald* XXXVI (September 23, 1943), pp. 538-539.

Suderman, Jacob, "The Origin of Mennonite State Service in Russia, 1870-1880" *Mennonite Quarterly Review* XVII (January 1943), pp. 23-47.

Tolles, Frederick B., "Can We Use Conscientious Objectors Wisely?" *Forum* (March 1946), pp. 585-589.

Wilcher, Denny, "Shall the C.P.S. Camps Continue?" *Christian Century*, LIX (December 16, 1942), pp. 1556-1559.

Yoder, John H., "The Unique Role of the Historic Peace Churches," *Brethren Life and Thought* XIV (Summer 1969), pp. 132-149.

Index

170

The Authors

Albert N. Keim grew up in an Amish community in Ohio. He is the oldest in a family of nine children. One of his early memories is of his father (an Amish bishop) returning from a visit to a Civilian Public Service camp to fellowship with young Amishmen at the camp

In 1955, as a 19-year-old, Keim was drafted and served as a Mennonite Central Committee PAX worker in a rebuilding project in Europe. He graduated from Eastern Mennonite College with a history degree in 1963. After earning an M.A. in medieval studies at the University of Virginia, he returned to teach history at Eastern Mennonite College in 1965. In 1971 he completed a Ph.D. at Ohio State. His dissertation research focused on the work of John

Foster Dulles as a churchman during the decade of the 1940s prior to becoming Secretary of State under Eisenhower.

His *Compulsory Education and the Amish* was published in 1975. It is a review of the issues and events leading to the *Yoder v. Wisconsin* Supreme Court case in 1972. In 1987 he edited the second volume of the Mennonite Experience in America history series.

Grant M. Stoltzfus was born in 1916 at Elverson, Pennsylvania, the fifth of six children. He graduated from Goshen College (B.A.), University of Pittsburgh (M.A.), Union Theological Seminary, Richmond, Virginia (B.D. and Th.D.), and served the church widely as a historian, teacher, writer, editor, and speaker.

He was publicity director at Akron, Pennsylvania (1941-1943) and, as a draftee, was administrator of Civilian Public Service units for Mennonite Central Committee (1943-1945) at Hagerstown, Maryland and Woodbine, New Jersey. He also served as a writer at the National Mental Health Foundation, Philadelphia, Pennsylvania (1945-1946). He edited *The Mennonite Community* magazine (1947-1953), wrote

Mennonites of the Ohio and Eastern Conference (Herald Press, 1969), served on the Historical Committee of the Mennonite Church, and taught at Eastern Mennonite College and Seminary (1957-1974). With his wife, Ruth Brunk Stoltzfus, he frequently spoke at family life conferences. Together they raised a family of two sons and three daughters.

Stoltzfus pioneered in recovering the early history of the Old Order Amish in colonial Pennsylvania. He was active in the National Committee for Amish Religious Freedom and the civil rights movement in Virginia. His concern for religious freedom and civil liberties inspired his work for conscientious objectors and the mentally handicapped during World War II. He was working on *The Politics of Conscience* at the time of his death in 1974. His widow is a speaker, writer, and broadcaster living at Harrisonburg, Virginia.